Managing Technology in the Operations Function

Butterworth-Heinemann – The Securities Institute
A publishing partnership

About the securities institute

Formed in 1992 with the support of the Bank of England, the London Stock Exchange, the Financial Services Authority, LIFFE and other leading financial organizations, the Securities Institute is the professional body for practitioners working in securities, investment management, corporate finance, derivatives and related businesses. Their purpose is to set and maintain professional standards through membership, qualifications, training and continuing learning and publications. The Institute promotes excellence in matters of integrity, ethics and competence.

About the series

Butterworth-Heinemann is pleased to be the official **Publishing Partner** of the the Securities Institute with the development of professional level books for: Brokers/ Traders; Actuaries; Consultants; Asset Managers; Regulators; Central Bankers; Treasury Officials; Compliance Officers; Legal Departments; Corporate Treasures; Operations Managers; Portfolio Managers; Investment Bankers; Hedge Fund Mangers; Investment Managers; Analysts and Internal Auditors, in the areas of: Portfolio Management; Advanced Investment Management; Investment Management Models; Financial Analysis; Risk Analysis and Management; Capital Markets; Bonds; Gilts; Swaps; Repos; Futures; Options; Foreign Exchange; Treasury Operations.

Series titles

■ **Professional Reference Series**
The Bond and Money Markets: *Strategy, Trading, Analysis*

■ **Global Capital Markets Series**
The REPO Handbook
Foreign Exchange and Money Markets: *Theory, Practice and Risk Management*
IPO and Equity Offerings
European Securities Markets Infrastructure
Best Execution in the Integrated Securities Market

■ **Operations Management Series**
Clearing, Settlement and Custody
Controls, Procedures and Risk
Relationship and Resource Management in Operations
Managing Technology in the Operations Function
Regulation and Compliance in Operations
Understanding the Markets

For more information
For more information on **The Securities Institute** please visit their web site:

www.securities-institute.org.uk

and for details of all **Butterworth-Heinemann Finance** titles please visit Butterworth-Heinemann:

www.bh.com/finance

Managing Technology in the Operations Function

David Loader and Graeme Biggs

OXFORD   AMSTERDAM   BOSTON   LONDON   NEW YORK   PARIS
SAN DIEGO   SAN FRANCISCO   SINGAPORE   SYDNEY   TOKYO

Butterworth-Heinemann
An imprint of Elsevier Science
Linacre House, Jordan Hill, Oxford OX2 8DP
200 Wheeler Road, Burlington MA 01803

First published 2002

British Library Cataloguing in Publication Data
Loader, David
  Managing technology in the operations function. –
  (Operations management series)
  1. Financial services industry – Management   2. Information
  technology – Management   3. Financial services industry –
  Data processing
  I. Title   II. Biggs, Graeme
  332.1'068

Library of Congress Cataloguing in Publication Data
A catalogue record for this book is available from the Library of Congress

ISBN 0 7506 5485 6

For information on all Butterworth-Heinemann finance publications
visit our website at www.bh.com/finance

Composition by Genesis Typesetting Limited, Rochester, Kent
Printed and bound in Great Britain

Contents

Preface

The use of technology in the financial markets is the key to the growth in the volumes of business. Without the advances in technology providing everything from electronic trading systems to Internet banking there would be no globalization of activity and no large, global investment banks. The impact that technology has had and is still having on the operations function is truly substantial. Paper has been drastically reduced or eradicated from the settlement and clearing processes. Significant amounts of information and instructions are sent electronically and today the crucial areas of control and risk management are heavily dependent on electronically generated data.

Of course, technology itself has presented many new challenges. Re-engineering of the functions and processes within businesses was a massive project. Procedures needed changing and adapting. Retraining was often businesswide and the implementation of systems often created logistical and budget problems. The end-products, however, are globalized operations functions, direct system links with counterparties including clients for distribution of data and remote clearing and settlement as the need to maintain a physical presence where the market is located is no longer a necessity.

It is difficult to imagine what the Operations area of twenty years ago looked like – still heavily paper-intensive, with prolonged processes and high levels of manual work. The processes that were automated relied on batch processing and required lengthy time windows to undertake the task. Naturally the clearing and settlement function worked within these constraints and so did the markets. The ability to handle increased activity was primarily about the capacity to take on additional people so it is not surprising that the costs associated with securities transactions were high.

In the industry today the use of technology reaches just about every aspect of the business. Electronic trading, messaging systems and information distribution have created a global market that is, relatively speaking, instantly accessible and available.

For operations this manifests itself in two ways. First, there is the automation of processes and second, the automation of information gathering and distribution. The impact of this has been to change the operations structure and procedures so that new functions could be introduced to deal with the new products being developed in the marketplace and, of course, the globalization of the industry and the resultant cross-border transactions. For the Operations managers this period of change has elevated the function from a pure support service into a dynamic revenue protector/generator with a heavy client service and risk management focus.

The reliance on technology to drive this progression forward and to meet the challenge is therefore a crucial consideration for the manager. As the markets continue to develop with significant speed in some cases, the need to identify the technology solutions and then to implement the technology is vitally important. Major projects like STP are often running alongside more fundamental system issues. Reliability and capacity issues and capability to handle new products are creating the scenario where systems are needing upgrading and, increasingly, replacement.

Getting the system that delivers the tools the manager and the Operations team needs is not an easy task. It is often made more difficult because of the gap between the technology providers, technical knowledge of system and their understanding of the operational environment as well as the Operations managers' gap between the knowledge of the operational environment and the technical knowledge of systems.

Numerous problems in most operations would not exist if those using the system better understood the scope and capability of the systems. Equally, systems would more closely meet the operational needs if programmers and developers understood the environment in which the systems would be operating. The most successful businesses are those where the power of technology is not only recognized but is then harnessed through a close relationship between the developers and users of the technology.

The challenge for the Operations teams and managers is to embrace technology and maximize this vital and powerful tool's use within the business. A failure to do so will inevitably have a negative impact on the Operations function and will ultimately damage the whole business.

In this book we look at aspects of managing technology that will help to achieve these goals.

Chapter 1

Key drivers for automation

Background

Historically the investment banking community has been slow to automate its administration functions. To take the UK as an example, prior to the 'Big Bang' in October 1986 share trading took place within the confines of what has often been described as a 'cosy honourable gentleman's club'. With a limited number of jobbers (market makers) and brokers executing trades through the physical exchange of paper slips on the stock exchange floor, transaction volumes were limited by the constraints of the trading mechanism. Add to this the fortnightly account period for settlement which entailed the physical exchange of stock certificates and stock transfer forms for banker's drafts, one can see this was not a business that readily lent itself to computerization. Stockbroking was a low transaction volume business conducted between a small number of participants geographically located in the one square mile that is the City of London. Coupled with the necessity for face-to-face execution of orders and the physical delivery of paper documentation and cheques, it would have been virtually impossible to gain significant benefit from the automation of such a physically intensive process.

By comparison, the retail banks and insurance companies, with their millions of retail customers geographically distributed across the UK (and in some cases beyond), were well advanced along the path of automation. Typical of the functions already highly automated by these two industries at the time were the production of insurance-renewal notices and bank statements which would be printed off in their tens of thousands, automatically enveloped and sent out to customers every month. With literally millions of customers, often with more than one policy or account, the drivers for automation in this area were abundantly clear. The insurers and retail banks, along with a number of other industries, particularly the utilities, were already well down the road of automation, forced into it by the huge volume of repetitive processes to be carried out in a limited time. Pre-October 1986, large transaction volumes were not a feature of UK capital markets.

For automation to be effective the underlying business processes must be suited to electronic computerized processing and there must be a tangible benefit to be gained from the IT investment. Before October 1986 in the UK, the underlying business process involving face-to-face dealing on the floor of the London Stock Exchange, the physical exchange of share certificates and hand-signed stock transfer forms clearly did not lend itself to electronic processing. On top of this, the low volumes were not giving rise to any capacity problems so there was no particular pressure to try to automate the process as it stood or to change the underlying process to facilitate automation.

By contrast, the production and distribution of policies, bank statements, electricity bills, etc. requiring no exchange of documents or signature authentication is a process that can readily be implemented in an electronic record-keeping environment and volumes are a clear driver to automate. Neither of these attributes were features of the UK capital markets before October 1986 and it was not until electronic trading was introduced that the UK securities market was really able to invest in technology leading to the levels of automation we see today.

The rest of this chapter looks at the significant changes in the capital markets that have had, or will have, an influence on the level of automation desired by the back offices of the various participants of the global capital markets. The first section, *Historical drivers of automation*, looks back at the key changes in the industry which have enabled the business to be automated and the drivers that have encouraged firms to invest in sophisticated IT solutions. The second section, *Industry challenges today*, describes changes that will force the pace and complexity of automation even more than we have already seen. It examines some specific issues and the impact they will have on processes and systems. The third section, *Internal pressures*, considers automation from the internal perspective of individual firms. While many of the industry changes leave firms little choice but to comply with requisite levels of automation, there are many internal issues that demand, what are often, even more complex levels of technology! Although not mandatory in terms of needing to adhere to an external operational interface, computerization is often the means to achieve a goal that is equally critical to the wellbeing of the business. It examines some of those internal requirements for which computerization of the underlying business process is a prerequisite to meeting the end objective.

Historical drivers of automation

Increasing transaction volumes

Between 1990 and 2001, annual trading volumes on the US stock markets rose from 83 billion to 841 billion shares, more than a tenfold increase. Over a similar period, volumes on the London Stock Exchange quadrupled. This has been a common story across the world's major markets but this year-on-year increase has created an ever-increasing burden for the back offices of broker/dealers, fund managers and custodians alike. As the world's stock exchanges moved to real-time screen-based trading so the dealing rooms of the global broker/dealers had to become more technologically sophisticated to keep pace. This increased level of sophistication in the dealing rooms made it possible for broker/dealers to execute even greater numbers of transactions than would have otherwise been possible with lesser technology. The much wider accessibility of real-time price information coupled with smaller spreads and commissions was enough to stimulate greater stock market activity even before considering the economic changes, like pension reform, that were contributing to a fundamental growth in transaction volumes. Unfortunately, while high-tech front-office systems facilitated trade execution at the press of a button, the back office was left to shift ever-increasing mounds of paper.

Initially the higher volumes were handled by a combination of late-night working and additional staff. However, with such a labour-intensive process, the additional labour required was directly proportional to the volume of trades, so as volumes kept rising labour became more expensive as did the office space required to accommodate it. The problem was that while the trading platforms had become highly automated, the clearing and settlement infrastructures remained largely paper based and consequently began to creak under the higher volumes, giving rise to increased settlement risk. One of the first examples of this strain was seen in the post-war stock market boom of the 1960s when the clearing and settlement process in the USA began to come to a halt under the sheer volume of paper. The problem became so serious that trading hours were shortened and the markets had to close one day per week to allow clearing and settlement to catch up. As a result of this rather embarrassing crisis, the market rallied together and in 1973 created the Depository Trust Company (DTC) as the central securities depository and settlement system. It was the immobilization of paper and the introduction of electronic trade confirmation, through the Institutional Delivery (ID) system, that gave the USA a head-start on the rest of the world. This provided the necessary infrastructure that encouraged market participants to invest in back-office technology and achieve the levels of efficiency many markets are still trying to reach today. There can be little doubt that settlement efficiency has been a key factor in the phenomenal growth of trading volumes on the US stock markets as without it, they would have come to a halt long ago just as they almost did in the 1960s.

Rolling settlement

While securities were represented in a physical form, transfer of ownership had to take place via a face-to-face meeting between buyer and seller where securities were exchanged for money. Because of the necessity for face-to-face meetings it made more sense for buyers and sellers to meet in one central location at a predetermined time in order that they could settle all their purchases and sales with the various counterparts all in one session. Often the purchase of securities from one counterpart would have been sold on to another so it was important for all three to be present in the same place at the same time. In order to facilitate this central gathering, physical markets normally used to work on a fixed settlement-day calendar. For example, in the UK until July 1993, all trades conducted between Monday and Friday were settled on the second Monday following the end of the trading period. In France, they followed a month-end settlement cycle that continued right up until October 2000, long after securities had been dematerialized. Even then, the local participants required a good deal of persuasion to convince them of the benefits of moving to rolling settlement.

Account period settlement, as it was known, was very convenient for Operations departments as it allowed them plenty of time to confirm all the trade details, prepare the necessary documentation and calculate funding requirements. Furthermore, because of the gap between the close of the trading period and the settlement day, they basically had a 'frozen' position with which to work for up to a month depending on jurisdiction. More importantly it provided more time to manage large peaks in activity, which in a manual environment was essential. Given a peak day's trading activity, you would, in some markets, have up to a month during which to spread the processing load. You effectively received advance notice of peak volumes and could therefore manage the settlement load accordingly. Although the period around settlement day was obviously busy, all the problems such as trade disputes, price differences, funding, etc. should have already been cleared up leaving only the actual exchange process itself to contend with. It was not, however, so popular with the credit departments who saw very large exposures build up with counterparts during the extended account period which could lead to restrictions being imposed to prevent limits being breached.

Once in a rolling settlement environment, even if it is not that short, everything becomes much more complex and time critical which is why we have had to look to automation. It is worth considering just a few aspects of the settlement process to appreciate the impact of rolling versus account period settlement.

Funding

In a rolling settlement environment you are funding for securities settlements every day whereas under an account period settlement you only need to fund for the periodic settlement day, be that monthly, fortnightly, etc. Not only are you funding every day but you may have only one day in which to calculate your requirements. Under a T+3 cycle you need to arrange FX cover by early afternoon on T+1 for availability on T+3 (FX settles T+2), assuming it's in a similar time zone. If the settlement time zone is east of your home one, you may need to calculate your position on T to put in an overnight spot FX order for execution on T+1.

You can see that as you move to rolling settlement, the whole process becomes much more fluid with balance forecasts moving continuously. Not only do you need to issue confirmations and settlement instructions on a more timely basis, you also need to ensure the transactional data is fed through to your cash-funding ladders as soon as possible to give the Treasury accurate information and sufficient time to arrange cover for T+3. It is only through systematization of the transaction process that the necessary levels of accuracy, timeliness and rapid dissemination of constantly changing information can be achieved.

Depo management

Reconciliation of settled depo positions becomes more critical but at the same time more difficult. You need to be managing your forecast forward depo position in line with the settlement cycle so that realignments or borrowings can be arranged, and to prevent erroneous delivery of clients' short positions. Because this needs to be done on a rolling daily basis, it is therefore necessary to run daily depo reconciliations if your forecast positions are to have any integrity. This is particularly time sensitive as agents tend to report settled positions overnight, losing you a day before you've even started. In all but the smallest firms it would just not be feasible to reconcile depo positions on a continuous rolling daily basis without some serious technology support. Under the account period regime, you could only reconcile as at the account period settlement days, when the vast bulk of the movements took place, so you had the luxury of time and a relatively static balance with which to reconcile.

Rolling settlement also puts increased pressure on the Corporate Actions desk who have to monitor record date positions every day rather than just on the account period settlement day.

Figure 1.1 shows that in an account period settlement regime you have a period between the end of the trading period and the

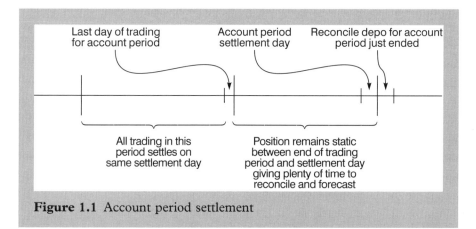

Figure 1.1 Account period settlement

settlement day for that account period where positions remain static and the necessary preparations for settlement can be made.

Figure 1.2 illustrates how in a rolling environment settlement occurs daily and therefore requires a much greater level of sophistication to monitor and accurately forecast settlement-day positions. Also, because we are having to forecast daily, we consequently have to reconcile daily to ensure a sound basis on which to make the forecasts.

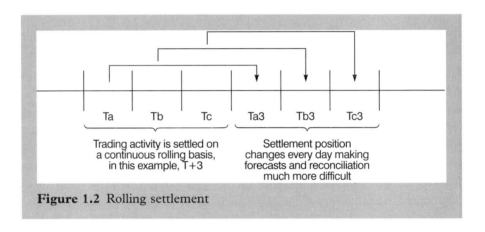

Figure 1.2 Rolling settlement

Nostro management

Similar to the depo, you also need to know your daily settled cash position in order to run your cash ladders, from which you can derive your funding requirements. Again, rolling settlement forces you into daily cash reconciliations, which can only be achieved with a highly automated matching engine with good exceptional tracking and reporting.

Dematerialization

While a significant amount of automation has been apparent in physical markets, the efficiency gains have always been limited by the number of people necessary to verify and collate the mounds of paperwork. As mentioned earlier, in a physical environment, it is mostly the tracking of physical paper and maintenance of positions which is computerized but this entails additional manual entry of the necessary status information, thus potentially increasing the cost of using automated solutions. The Indian market in the 1990s was a good example of a very physical market (certificates used to arrive by the lorry-load) which at the same time made extensive use of technology to track and control the mountains of paper. Although the custodians invested heavily in technology to cope with the rapid influx of foreign investment, they still had to maintain armies of settlement staff to physically count, check, sign, etc. the underlying paper records of legal title. This was a prime example of leading-edge technology but not effective automation. In this case it was the underlying clearing infrastructure that needed changing before real efficiencies could be gained.

It is only when a market dematerializes that not only can real automation be achieved but it will actually be forced upon the participants. As physical documented proof of ownership is converted into electronic book entry form at the Central Securities Depositories (CSDs) so the true benefits of automation can be realized. In a paperless environment it is essential that firms maintain robust and accurate records of their book entry holdings held with the depository as there is no longer any absolute proof of title other than the electronic records of the CSDs. The incentive to automate suddenly becomes that much greater. On the one hand, firms are forced into maintaining their own computerized records of holdings to replace the physical certificates and, on the other, no longer have the processing flow interrupted by the physical handling of certificates and stock transfer forms, etc.

Furthermore, CSDs and regulators generally insist on minimum levels of technological sophistication from their members to be sure that the clearing and settlement process is not disrupted by poor performance on the part of individual participants. They are therefore very keen to ensure that members have a level of sophistication and automation comparable to their own systems so that they can operate at the same speed and levels of consistency as the rest of the market. As participants are effectively interconnected to each other through the CSD hub any failure by one member could easily have a catastrophic impact on the rest of the system. Unlike a manual system where an operational failure may affect a handful of transactions, a failure in an automated system is likely to result in many hundreds or thousands of transactions being impacted causing a massive knock-on effect throughout the system.

Program trading

The move towards sector-based investment strategies, the development of equity indices and their associated tracker funds has led to a massive growth in program trading activity to the point where it is now common in most fund managers and broker/dealers. Alongside this there are arbitrageurs generating thousands of trades or more per day as they go in and out of the market to exploit pricing anomalies. The nature of the business requires trades to be kept small in value, to avoid impacting the arbitrage opportunity but large in number to generate material profit. However, as every small trade has to be settled individually (excluding net settlement markets), clearing costs become a significant factor in the profitability of the business. The program trading business puts enormous pressure on the back office not only to cope with large volumes but to do so at minimum cost. This business demands extremely high levels of STP so that traders are not constrained by volume limits and should actually see a unit cost reduction as volumes increase. They should only be picking up the fixed costs of the system irrespective of how much volume they push through it. So the more they trade, the cheaper it gets. The agent banks' clearing costs are also an important factor and similarly need to be reduced to a minimum. While discounted tariffs can be negotiated for increased volume, real savings will only come if you can provide settlement instructions in a form and consistency that your CSD or agent can also process without manual intervention. It is now common to negotiate a very low unit cost with severe penalties for instructions requiring manual intervention on the part of the CSD or agent bank. In order to work to such a tariff structure you will need comprehensive reference databases combined with intelligent default rules to ensure accuracy of transaction reference information on a consistent basis. The prospect of handling such high volumes to this level of quality and consistency in a manual environment is not a practical proposition.

Program trading has had a significant influence on the pace and level of automation in the whole post-execution environment and continues to exert pressure on the clearing and settlement cost base. As the number of trading platforms increase, at least in the medium term, the opportunity for arbitrageurs is also likely to increase but the opportunities will have to be exploited with increasingly higher volumes as the arbitrage margin becomes smaller and smaller.

Cross-border trading

The growth in cross-border trading activity, particularly at the time-zone extremities, has put the whole trade booking, confirmation and settlement process under severe time constraints. Consider a trade executed on the Tokyo Stock Exchange on a Monday morning. By the time the London client has confirmation, the trade date in Tokyo has almost ended before it can be affirmed. If there is any problem with the execution, the Tokyo broker won't get to hear of it until T+1 and will have to wait until the end of T+1 before he can liaise with the London client to resolve the problem. Assuming the problem is resolved first time, it is still going to be T+2 before the Tokyo agent bank receives a settlement instruction leaving him very little time to pre-match and clear up any problems in time for settlement on T+3. With any sort of volume this would not be achievable in a manual environment so it was essential that any European-based client trading in Asia have good levels of automation to work within the highly compressed settlement times frames. For US-based clients investing in Asia the time-zone compression effect is obviously even greater.

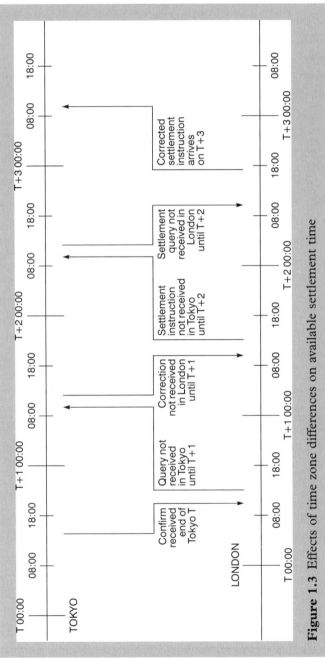

Figure 1.3 Effects of time zone differences on available settlement time

Figure 1.3 illustrates the more extreme effects of time zones on settlement cycles but even the loss of a couple of hours across the European markets can be significant particularly when volumes are high and things are not going as smoothly as one would like. Furthermore, with Operations departments routinely transacting business in upwards of thirty markets, it can be difficult for staff to remember and prioritize their work according to all the different deadlines creeping up on them throughout the day.

Certainly until recently, all cross-border settlement activity in the local market was handled by the agent bank intermediary reducing the effective clearing window even further. So even before we start worrying about time-zone compression of the settlement cycle, the local intermediary has already brought forward the cut-off point for settlement by the amount of time he requires to process the client's settlement instruction. As a minimum the clearing bank will have to receive the instruction, which may be a fax, into a secure system, verify its authenticity, apply some basic validation checks and, if necessary, repair it by corresponding with the originating client. This may require the resending of a corrected instruction, depending on the nature of the problem, which itself will then have to be recycled through the whole process again before being accepted as an authentic, valid instruction upon which the agent can act in good faith. Next, the agent will check the instruction against settled positions and other pending instructions for the same value date before telephone pre-matching the instruction with the counterpart's agent bank. Only then will he be in a position to release the instruction into the local CSD. Before agent banks were able to automate much of this process, it was not unusual for them to require the client's settlement instruction at least one full day before settlement day. In some markets they would need it even earlier as the local CSD might require the agent bank's instruction to be in the system on the evening before settlement day.

It is clear that even with quite relaxed settlement cycles, the combination of time-zone difference and the interposition of an intermediary leave very little room for error or delay. There was, therefore, a massive incentive for anyone involved with cross-border trading to automate everything they possibly could to keep errors and delays to an absolute minimum so that the limited time available could be used to address what should be a much smaller number of genuine issues. From the agent banks' perspective this was very difficult because they had to contend with the wide variation in formats and quality of instructions received from their clients. Similarly clients were dependent on an almost as widely varying format and quality of settlement confirmations for their automatic posting of settled trades. In the absence of a common standard, clearing banks developed their own proprietary communications interfaces for the transmission of settlement instructions and settlement confirmations but this proved very expensive for investors who found themselves having to support almost as many different interfaces as they had clearing banks. Even so, investors had little choice but to build and maintain bespoke interfaces to their clearing banks at least in high-volume markets. In some ways the proprietary interfaces worked in the banks' favour as it made it very difficult for investors to change their relationships because of the high cost of redeveloping another bespoke interface for the newly appointed clearer. On the downside, smaller clients whose volumes could not justify the development of multiple bespoke interfaces continued to send various forms of manual instruction along with the con-sequential variation in quality. As we will see in the next section, things could not advance too much until a universal communications media and data-formatting standard could be adopted by the industry as a whole.

A secure inter-bank communication medium

As mentioned earlier, the main cash-clearing banks were automating long before the securities industry to keep up with the rapid increase in worldwide payment volumes. They soon realized that if they were to be able to automate effectively, they had to come up with a universal standard for inter-bank communications irrespective of where the banks resided. Until this time, all inter-bank payments had to be made manually by tested telex as this was the only communication medium with worldwide coverage and standards. Telex was designed for communication of free-format text and so could not be adapted for computer-to-computer communication. It was therefore apparent to the banks that they would have to develop their own secure payments communication network if they were to stand any chance of automating payments processing across globally distributed organizations. The result was the formation of the Society for Worldwide Inter-bank Financial Telecommunications (SWIFT) in 1973, a market cooperative owned by the member banks, and the transmission of the first payment instructions in 1977. The SWIFT Fin network experienced rapid growth with traffic volumes increasing every year since then as more banks and more countries came on-stream. However, it was not until 1987 that the banks, who owned and controlled SWIFT, at the time, opened the doors to the broker/dealer and fund manager community. SWIFT was now set to become the *defacto* communications medium for securities messages.

Securities are a much more complex financial instrument than cash to process. There are an enormous number of them compared to the relatively small number of currencies, they settle according to different cycles, have specific registration names, do not have unique identifiers, have different units of quantity to mention but a few of their many peculiarities. Because of the vagaries and inconsistency of the securities instrument and its associated settlement procedure the first SWIFT securities message formats were kept flexible to accommodate all eventualities. Although in a structured format (field tag concept), the field contents themselves were mostly unvalidated free format text apart from a few key identifier and date fields. There has been much criticism over the years about the lack of standards and validation applied to the securities messages, but one should bear in mind that the messages were originally designed as much for manual completion and interpretation as they were for computerized processing. However, at worst, it provided a faster, more secure alternative communication medium to the ageing telex network and, at best, facilitated the development of generic computer-to-computer communication for the clearing and settlement of securities. Much effort went into developing message standards and country-specific guidance notes, mainly by the custodian banks, and by working closely with their clients, STP rates of up to 100% could be achieved in rare cases. A consequence of these high STP levels was to put enormous pressure on clearing fees. Broker/dealers in particular were keen to get some payback on their investment and argued that as the agent banks were now enjoying fully automated hands-off processing, they could no longer justify their existing fee tariffs. What developed was a new tariff structure with much lower fees for STP trades but an additional punitive levy for exceptions and repairs.

Because all the agent banks were already on SWIFT for payments, it was not a very large step for them to develop a securities-processing capability which they hoped would provide the same level of automation to their securities clearing and settlement processing as they enjoyed in the payments business. For the broker/dealers and fund managers it gave them the chance to use a single uniform technological interface across all their clearing relationships. Now that they had a common interface, it was much easier to justify spending on more sophisticated technology because you only needed to do it once and it could be deployed in all markets.

Although much was achieved with the ISO 7775 message standard, eventually its lack of standards, its fixed message structures and lack of validation proved to be a limiting factor on the degree of STP that could be achieved. Because of the difficulty in getting messages changed (just imagine the number of people and systems affected for the smallest change) firms started to code more and more information into free-format fields, normally agreed on a bilateral basis, in order to satisfy changing business requirements. While this method was effective for the two bilateral parties, the interface was, as a result, becoming less and less generic, not at the message level but at the field content level. The consequence of this was that changing agent bank relationship would require a degree of tinkering with the

SWIFT interface to meet the new bank's requirements – not quite the generic medium that was needed. This culminated in the development of a new message standard, ISO 15022, which, because it is based on a data dictionary principle, allows structured fields to be added without having to change the whole message format each time. This new standard will allow firms to reach an even higher level of STP and eliminate many of the exceptions that occurred under the ISO 7775 standard due to its inability to define data at a low enough level of granularity.

Staff costs

In spite of the high salaries relative to many other industries, the securities industry still struggles to find and retain good-quality staff in the Operations area. Traditionally Operations has not been viewed as one of the more interesting areas of the business and many graduate entrants see Operations only as a gateway to greater things. Operations is a difficult function to resource as it contains such a wide variety of duties, some of which can be extremely complex and others that are positively mundane. However, although there are certainly still a lot of routine jobs, all of which are critical to the wellbeing of the organization, they are also full of complex exceptions that require considerable skill and, more importantly, experience to handle effectively. Staff capable of dealing with the more complex exceptions can soon become bored with the more mundane side of the job making it very difficult to retain the necessary calibre of staff in these roles.

A further aggravation is the very large volatility in business activity experienced by most firms in the securities industry and the volume sensitivity in staffing levels. When volumes are up, everyone is recruiting for the same resources, pushing up salaries further and leaving large gaps in experience as people move on. Not only is this very expensive for the industry (salary levels do not normally fall) it also creates unnecessary risk at the very time when business is booming and skills and experience are most badly needed.

Automation has often been viewed as the solution to this problem by creating a 'factory' environment where the few manual processes that remain are completely routine and can be covered by lower-calibre staff. This production line environment should allow resources to be brought in at short notice, with little or no experience and consequently at much lower cost. Unfortunately, even after millions of pounds' of investment in advanced technology, staffing continues to be an issue for most Operations departments, so why hasn't technology solved the staff problem?

There is no doubt that technology has had a significant impact on Operations staff numbers although much of this saving has been more than used up by growth in volume – nonetheless still a significant saving. The majority of these savings have taken place in what were the 'production line' processes such as confirmation production, settlement instruction, etc. which were relatively easy to automate. To make further savings through the application of technology is proving increasingly difficult and we will now look at some of the reasons for this.

While many functions have been automated, the 80/20 rule plays a key part in limiting the amount of resources that can be saved by nearly always leaving a residual 20% of the task to be picked up manually. This 20% will be made up of various pieces of the process including those functions that were de-scoped to prevent further cost/time overruns, those low-volume functions deemed to be not worth automating and the exceptions that do not fit neatly into a systematized solution. To make matters worse, business circumstances often conspire to magnify the size of the 20% so that, in practice, it requires, say, 40% of the staff to cover it. Typically the parts de-scoped are the more complex, high-risk areas that demand extensive checking and rigorous controls, the low-volume problem becomes high volume and the exceptions increase proportionately with the overall volumes. This residue, because of its critical and unpredictable nature, demands the highest skilled, most experienced staff who are also the most expensive. So while it is an exaggeration, for the sake of example, the cost savings on the 60% of staff headcount may only account for 50% of the cost. Many Operations departments find themselves at this juncture, where the 80% has been automated but the remainder of staff costs are tied up in the complex or ill-defined processes of the residual 20%. Pressure continues to be exerted on staff costs but it is very difficult to achieve significant savings in headcount across what, in many organizations, has become a diverse and fragmented inventory of manual duties. At the same time, the cost of further automation is much higher, due to the complex and vague nature of the processes and the cost–benefit is reduced due to the smaller numbers of staff that can be saved each time.

Although this sounds quite negative, it is important to recognize the law of diminishing returns coming into play. Excluding hardware and any additional system software, as you get increasingly closer to achieving 100% automation of any particular task, so the more complex and expensive the application development will become and the more uncertain will be the cost–benefit. Figure 1.4 shows that to get from 75% to 100% automation is going to be significantly more expensive than getting from 25% to 50%.

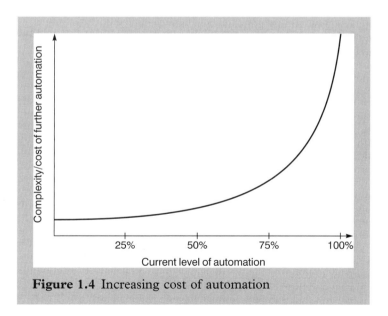

Figure 1.4 Increasing cost of automation

Summary

In this section we have looked back at the key drivers which have in combination not only enabled firms to automate but have actually forced them to. We saw earlier that while volumes, rolling settlement and time-zone constraints were demanding more efficient processing methods, the underlying market infrastructures requiring physical movement of paper and the lack of a universal secure communications medium imposed severe limitations on the level of automation that could be achieved. It is therefore clear that without all these factors, drivers and facilitators, the levels of automation we see today would never have been possible. The next section looks forward to examine where the new drivers and facilitators are coming from and the challenges faced in confronting them.

Industry challenges today

Having considered the historical factors influencing the pace and degree of automation in the securities industry to date, we are now going to look at what is driving it today and what is on the horizon. If we consider technology and automation generally across all industries, the first level of automation, while often having the greater impact on efficiency, is at the same time the most straightforward. We basically take the high-volume repetitive manual processes and 'simply' replicate them on a machine or computer. This initial step in the evolution of an industry, while we should not underestimate its achievements, is relatively simple and safe in that we have a tried and tested manual template on which to base it and, if necessary, fall back on. Technology simply enables us to deliver the same end result but hopefully in a quicker and cheaper way to a higher and more consistent quality. In many ways this is where the securities clearance and settlement world is today, i.e. we have automated, to a degree, a process that has been in operation for over a hundred years. Invariably the cost–benefit is very clear as it results in a direct and immediate reduction in labour costs and so the investment can easily be justified.

The next phase of evolution is much more interesting in that it enables us to do new things that probably hadn't even been thought of before and, even if they had, could certainly not have been achieved without a minimum level of automation. A good example is index arbitrage, where a whole basket of stocks, matching the index future, has to be purchased simultaneously with the sale of the future. As these indexes can contain as many as 500 stocks, it is easy to see that this business could not be done without the advent of electronic order routing and execution. Additionally, this technology-enabled business created previously unforeseen pressures on downstream systems which was certainly the case with program trading and the large volumes it generated for the back offices. As the level of computerization increases in the various links of the transaction chain, you may suddenly find you are faced with new processing problems that would not otherwise have existed. The solutions to these types of issues are more complex and the cost–benefit less clear because, without the benefit of hindsight, the level of uncertainty over how the process will work is so much greater. In the following sections we will look at some of these types of development as well as some of the more fundamental issues, such as increasing volume, that still continue to pose a challenge.

Transaction volume

According to the experts, securities trading volumes and equities in particular are set to increase year on year for many years to come. We can also see that the ongoing consolidation of both buy-and-sell side participants is concentrating volumes into fewer entities which in itself is causing individual firms' volumes to rise even before taking account of overall industry growth. Without going into the reason we can safely assume that most Operations departments can expect to see a significant growth in volume over the next 5 years. Indeed, firms not anticipating material growth in volume have in many ways a larger problem to contend with and one that is more difficult to solve. As we mentioned earlier, subsequent phases of industry maturity become increasingly complex and, consequently, technologically more expensive to address. We are no longer talking about simple automation of routine processes but rather about the challenge of keeping pace with all the other changes discussed later. Small to medium-sized houses will need a minimum critical volume to give them an economic cost per trade. The cost of developing a CREST interface, for example, is much the same whether you are going to use it for 1000 trades or 10 000 trades per day. The ongoing IT support costs will also be the same so the firm who performs only 1000 trades per day is going to have a system cost per trade ten times higher than the firm with 10 000 trades per day. This difference in unit cost can have a large impact on the business and can render some small margin trading businesses non-viable.

This is where the volume issue starts to become interesting. Having suggested that volume is a necessity to achieve the required economy of scale, this argument is only applicable to the technology side of the equation. Increasing volumes, no matter how well automated, will still be an issue for the Operations department. We have a conundrum, IT needs high volumes to be efficient and Operations work better with lower volumes (to a limit). We will now look in more detail at how the combination of automation and high volumes affects the Operation area and what can be done to ease the burden.

For the purposes of this exercise we'll assume our Operations department enjoys STP rates from trade capture to despatch of settlement instruction of, say, 80%. Assume there are five staff handling 5000 trades per day – in fact they are handling only 1000 trades because the others are not even seen. If volumes were to double and the same level of STP was maintained (in practice it is likely to improve as the higher volumes tend to be generated in the more automated business lines) we would need to double our staff to 10. For a doubling in volume, we have seen a doubling in staff but only an incremental increase of five. If, however, out STP rates were 0, taking a simplistic view, we would have 25 staff managing the 5000 trades per day but would need an additional 25 to handle 10 000 per

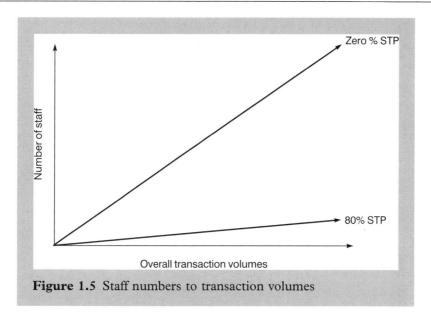

Figure 1.5 Staff numbers to transaction volumes

day – five times more than in the STP environment. So although for a given percentage increase in volume we need a similar percentage increase in staff, the absolute increase is much lower for high levels of STP (see Figure 1.5).

High levels of STP help to insulate the Operations area from trading volume volatility and the greater the level of STP, the greater the insulation. This is essential for a business like the securities industry, which is notoriously subject to large spikes in trading activity.

Another area that is generating significantly large increases in trading volumes is the growing trend to remote membership within the Euro zone. The large volumes are caused by two factors. First, institutional size orders are being placed directly on domestic exchanges along with the much smaller retail business. This results in the typically larger orders of remote institutions being matched (or split) against many smaller orders with ratios of 15 splits per order not being unheard of. What was once one trade with one local broker is now 15 trades with, depending on the exchange, a similar number of different counterparties. Hence the Operations area is affected by a greater number of counterparties together with greater volume. Second, the automatic order placement combined with the much cheaper cost per trade of remote membership facilitates new, small-margin arbitrage business that requires large volumes to generate material profit. Because these new arbitrage techniques are so dependent on precise timing of execution, they just would not have been possible with a domestic broker intermediary as any delay in order submission could cause the opportunity to be missed. This will be an ongoing trend as international broker/dealers develop more new businesses with narrower margins, which require the ability to execute large numbers of trades quickly and cheaply.

Trade confirmation

Over the past years there has been an enormous amount of attention paid to STP of the settlement part of the transaction chain. In particular the focus has been on trying to achieve a seamless interface between broker/dealer and local agent bank, between fund manager and global custodian and between the global custodian and their agent banks. To a large extent this has been driven by the global custodians who suffer more than most from a non-STP environment. Not only do they have to contend with the many varieties of settlement instruction formats received from their fund manager clients, they then have to forward them on to the appropriate agent bank, taking account of any particular formatting nuances they may have. While there is still a long way to go on the STP of the settlement leg, the framework for it is in place and there is a proven model to work to. However, it is just one part of the overall transaction chain from order placement to reconciliation and now the pressure is on to extend STP up the chain towards order routing and down the chain to final reconciliation. In this section we will look at how electronic trade confirmation (ETC) is influencing trade-processing technology.

Through its Depository Trust Company (DTC) the USA has been using electronic trade confirmation services since the launch of the

Institutional Delivery (ID) system in 1973. Not only was it providing electronic confirmation/affirmation services but it automatically fed a settlement instruction to the clearing system off the back of the confirmation, thus eliminating the possibility of differences between confirmation and settlement instruction.

However, while the ID system proved very effective in the US domestic market, it was not until much later that the cross-border issue was addressed. In 1991 a group of ten fund managers and broker/dealers met to form an Industry User Group (IUG) with a mandate to draw up the specification and select vendors to build and operate a cross-border ETC service. Thomson Financial ESG was one of the chosen vendors along with DTC, the London Stock Exchange and the International Securities Markets Association (ISMA). The latter two were to be subsumed by Thomson in 1996 leaving Thomson to dominate the cross-border ETC marketplace while DTC, with its Tradesuite product, dominated the US domestic market. However, the cross-border use of ETC has been slow to catch on and the vast majority of trades are still confirmed by telex and fax. As with any new, shared service, the problem has been achieving critical mass to justify the costs of implementing an ETC system. It is not unusual for fund managers to use as many as 100 broker/dealers so the chances of them all being on ETC is quite remote. As we saw earlier, automating only part of a service significantly reduces its cost-effectiveness because you still have to support the residual manual process and, in addition, now have to support the automated process as well. For many fund managers, unless they could use ETC across the board and completely eliminate rekeying and paper confirmations, it was not worth implementing at all as the cost–benefit was much less clear-cut. Furthermore, as it is typically the fund manager who owns the relationship and has his or her own reasons for using a particular broker/dealer, the ability of broker/dealers to support ETC did not figure highly in the selection process. It was the research, commission and market intelligence that dictated which broker/dealers would be used. However, with increasing competition and tighter margins fund managers started to look very carefully at their back-office costs and confirmations was an area where automation could provide significant savings. During the late 1990s, fund managers' back offices found themselves having a say in broker relationships in exchange for reduced operating costs and discovered that they were able to dictate the operational regime under which they are prepared to do business, even overriding the fund managers themselves. It is quite common now for larger fund managers to insist on their broker using electronic trade confirmation so that they can increase their internal STP rates and control costs. This has generated a much keener interest from brokers' front offices who now see their business dependent on a service that has traditionally been the domain of the back office. This is proving to be an interesting challenge because it extends the STP path right back up the transaction chain to the point of order placement requiring a more seamless and timely interface between front- and back-office systems. The processing from order receipt to despatch of confirmation crosses backwards and forwards between front- and back-office responsibilities and their systems as confirmations are sent and allocations received. This requires much closer coupling of the two systems' environments to support a greater level of data exchange to facilitate a robust and timely confirmation service.

Add to this the difference in communication message formats, FIX in the front office, SWIFT in the back, and it is apparent that the full automation of ETC presents quite a challenge (Figure 1.6). However, following the announcement in July 2001 that SWIFT and FIX Protocol Ltd (FPL) would seek convergence of their respective messaging protocols by the adoption of ISO 15022 XMP as an industry standard, the future does look more encouraging. The convergence of these two standards will not happen overnight because there is too much invested in the existing protocols, but over time, the joint standard will facilitate the unification of the pre-trade and trade world defined in FIX with the post-trade world according to SWIFT.

On a final note, many fund managers, apart from insisting on the use of ETC, are now monitoring confirmation performance of their

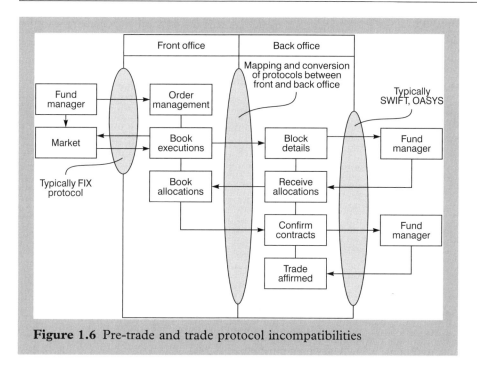

Figure 1.6 Pre-trade and trade protocol incompatibilities

broker/dealers and those who fall below the required threshold are automatically taken off the list of eligible broker/dealers – no questions asked. Now the broker/dealers' front offices are really becoming interested in the mundane world of confirmations!

Monitoring the automated environment

As Operations departments gradually move towards increasingly higher levels of automation, more and more of the business becomes invisible. On a positive note the equity operations manager does not notice the four S&P 500 baskets that went through between 3:00 and 3:15pm. However, what he also does not notice at 6:00 pm is that the confirmations are still sitting on one of the system queues waiting to go to the SWIFT terminal. Depending on the sophistication of the fund manager, the broker may already have been crossed off the list for failing to meet the service level on 2000 trades and that is in a STP environment!

The more automated a process becomes, the more it needs to be monitored. When a manual process breaks down, one or two transactions may be affected; when an automated process breaks down hundreds of trades are generally impacted. Regardless of who does it, the Operations department must make sure robust monitoring and escalation processes are in place throughout the whole life cycle of the transaction. Because of the number and diverse nature of the myriad systems components involved and the critical nature of the task, we find ourselves calling on technology again to solve our problems. It should be noted that what we are discussing here is the monitoring of system processes because it is these failures that will cause the most damage; manual processes will already have their own management control infrastructure in place.

When designing system monitors, you are monitoring not just for outright failure but also for any abnormal trend in processing throughput. The monitors must be designed to watch the progress of every trade through every major systems component until it arrives at its destination. This means ensuring that no trade is held up at any point in the processing chain for more than a predetermined amount of time; it is not sufficient to say 'I can see a steady flow of trades coming through' and assume all is well. It is a common mistake with distributed systems to assume that if you see a good flow of trades filtering through they are all getting through. Unfortunately this is not always the case. Because of the complexity of today's financial instruments and the terms under which they are traded, virtually every trade ends up associating itself with its own bespoke piece of processing software. In practice, every trade is subject to a unique combination of processes, any of which could fail independently or in combination, halting the progress of that particular trade through the system. As an example, all equity trades in all markets are flowing through the system except for the £50 million new issue trade which just happened to be for a new client with a specific commission structure for which the new calculation routine had failed! Isolated failures are very easily missed unless you have a systematized robust monitoring mechanism.

Off the back of this control and monitoring, it should be relatively easy to extract STP statistics as every break-point and exception queue in the system is being monitored. It is becoming increasingly important to be able to demonstrate your STP rates as it is perceived as a sign of quality and efficiency. There are even 'prestigious' industry awards for the best STP performers although the true measure of STP across firms is far from being an exact science. An interesting question is whether a failure of an automated process that has to be fixed by IT, but would have otherwise processed the trades automatically, should count as non-STP. And if it is classified as non-STP, how many trades would you count in the non-STP category? Perhaps a few thousand had been held up until it was fixed! It is still a fairly grey area as to what does and does not count as STP. This example raises a valid point in that Operations' definition of an 'exception' is basically something that falls out of the automated process flow because it was not designed to handle it in the first place. Operations will ensure the necessary alerts and manual procedures are in place to ensure these are picked up on an exceptional basis. However, failures in computerized processes themselves do not fall into our Operations definition of 'exceptions' because if it did, we would end up manually checking that automation was working – somewhat of a contradiction. Having explained that, we will now contradict ourselves and say that although system failures are not 'exceptions' in the sense they are something Operations have to contend with on a regular basis, they do need to be monitored as their consequences are more far-reaching. In the case of an outright failure it is obvious something is wrong and the necessary escalation procedures will be followed to ensure that it is addressed with the appropriate level of urgency. More likely is a degradation of service or an isolated failure, such as in the previous new issue example, which can easily go unnoticed and result in missed deadlines and broken service level agreements. In a high-STP environment it is essential than Operations is given the right system monitoring tools that can provide them with positive confirmation that all transactions are being processed to accepted service levels. In our experience, isolated system failures and gradual degradation of throughput are the most-common cause of missed deadlines in STP environments and should be monitored very closely.

Even shorter settlement cycles

According to studies by the TowerGroup, a leading research and advisory firm specializing in technology within the finance industry, the industry will spend $19 billion moving to a T+1 settlement cycle which begs the question, is it really necessary? According to the SIA business case for T+1 presented in 2000, the total value of US trades awaiting settlement on a daily average basis was over $375 billion. Based on a T+3 settlement cycle this means that on any one day there is over $1 trillion of outstanding settlement exposure. At current growth rates this figure will reach $2.8 trillion by 2004, a figure the authorities are clearly uncomfortable with. By reducing the settlement cycle to one day, this exposure can be reduced to nearer $1 trillion – quite a tempting proposition. The same SIA business case estimates the industry will save $2.7 billion annually, mainly derived from the more efficient clearing and settlement processes that will have to be implemented to achieve T+1. Canada, Australia, Brazil and Japan have already announced their intention to move to T+1 settlement at or around the same time as the USA, currently scheduled for 2005.

Some may think that the most difficult part was moving from fortnightly or monthly account settlement to T+3 rolling settlement and that the move from T+3 to T+1 looks trivial by comparison. In the UK, settlement moved from a 3-week calendar period to rolling T+10 in July 1993, T+5 in June 1995 but did not achieve T+3 until February 2001. It is interesting to note that the cycle was shrunk by 5 days in just two years but to reduce it by a further 2 days took another 6 years! One should point out that during those 6 years, stocks were dematerialized as settlement was migrated to CREST but it would still suggest the last move from T+5 to T+3 was much more of a challenge. The move to T+1 in

order of magnitude is more complex than anything that has gone
before and will require a complete re-engineering of the current
divide between trade and post-trade procedures into a single
unified process. To give you some idea of just how big this is, the
Securities Industry Association estimate getting to T+1 will cost
the industry $8 billion while the TowerGroup puts the figure at
around $19 billion (See Figure 1.7)

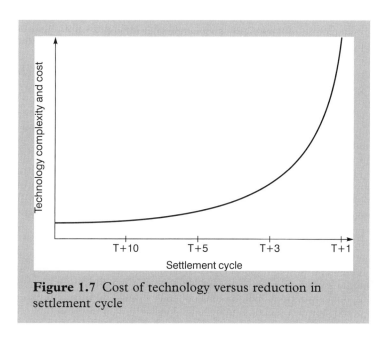

Figure 1.7 Cost of technology versus reduction in
settlement cycle

In the past, shortening settlement cycles have been addressed by a
combination of automation and additional staff to enable the usual
settlement problems to be followed up in the compressed time
frames. In a T+1 environment, you do not have time to clear up any
problems. Unless you are trade matched and locked in on T,
settlement is not going to take place on T+1, which basically means
that any problems must be prevented in the first place. It will require
a quality of static data, levels of STP and real-time processing the
likes of which few, if any, organizations can meet with their current
systems platforms.

In a T+1 environment, the post-execution, pre-settlement period, where problems are traditionally fixed, disappears – confirmation and settlement instruction become one and the same. There cannot be any room for errors to creep in between confirmation matching and despatch of settlement instruction and this is where GSTPA and OMGEO come in. Apart from providing a trade-matching engine, they can also forward the corresponding settlement instruction onto the custodian or even direct to the depository. As they are doing it for both sides of the trade, based on the information contained in the already matched confirmations, enriched where necessary by common reference data, there can be no settlement matching errors at the clearing agent or depository. Simple in concept but technically, regulatory and legally more difficult than certainly we can imagine! The industry has until 2005 to get it working.

It is not just a technology problem; there is also an interesting organizational issue for the Operations department. With confirmation and settlement matching being consolidated in to one of the global trade matching engines, who manages it within the Operations department; the settlements desk or the confirmations desk? In the current organizational set-up, the settlements desk would only ever deal with failed trades as there is no pre-settlement period in which to do anything. However, confirmations desks are currently focused on the economic terms of trades and the trading accounts – will they be able to understand problems in the settlement terms? As confirmation matching, settlement instruction and settlement pre-matching come together, so the organizational structure will need to change and staff retrained to work in a multidisciplinary environment. This unified confirmation and settlement function will require high-calibre staff who will find themselves dealing exclusively with exceptions under extreme pressures of time. They will require specialist knowledge and have an analytical approach that will allow them to resolve exceptions in a much-reduced timeframe. This profile is likely to be quite different from that of many staff currently working in Operations departments and will need to be addressed by management over the next few years.

Multiple-settlement locations

The proliferation of electronic stock exchanges and the competition between clearing houses and CSDs to provide clearing services has given rise to a new obstacle in the path towards settlement automation. Most systems have been developed on the basis that a given security generally has a default settlement location irrespective of where it is traded. Of course, when these rules were formulated, securities were always traded on their home exchange or OTC and, in either case, had to settle in their home clearing and settlement centre. When the 'international' exchanges were set up, they had no natural home in which to base the clearing of the transactions traded on their exchanges so they effectively put the settlement out to tender with the existing ICSDs and CSDs. In the early days it was the ICSDs who, with their existing links to the CSDs, were already well positioned to handle this international business and so they stole a considerable lead on the domestic CSDs. A good example was Tradepoint, who struck a deal with Euroclear to clear all its trades irrespective of home market. This was good news for the ICSDs as they saw themselves obtaining an increasingly larger share of the international exchanges' business so that eventually they would be achieving almost 100% internal book entry settlement without even going out to the domestic CSDs – a very lucrative business. Fearful of losing their home market to the ICSDs, the CSDs started to develop links to other CSDs in order to offer similar functionality to their own members, many of whom would not have sufficient credit status to join the ICSDs directly. CREST was very active in this area, establishing links with Sega-Intersettle as early as September 1999 to be followed by links to Clearstream and DTC. This offered CREST members the chance to trade on multiple international exchanges but settle and hold securities via their existing CREST interface. In order to enhance their attractiveness further, the international exchanges started to offer members a choice of settlement location so, for example, trades dealt on Virt-X can be settled in CREST, Euroclear or Sega-Intersettle. Suddenly, the settlement location has become a variable to be determined on a trade-by-trade basis depending on place of trade and, for broker/dealers, client preference.

As an example, an international broker/dealer buys Italian stock from a client on Virt-X who settles in Euroclear but has sold on to an Italian broker who settles in Monti Titoli. Not only does the broker have to contend with different settlement locations for the same stock, but he also has a long position in one location and a short position in the other which has to be realigned on or before settlement day. Add to this the additional effort for cash management and the cost of collateral to cover a long and short position and you begin to see that managing multiple settlement locations is a complex and costly business.

This issue gives rise to a need for more sophisticated settlement detail enrichment rules with the ability to override them on a case-by-case basis. As mentioned earlier, many systems were designed on the premise of one default settlement location per instrument and any variation was going to be an exception. But now, with the diversity of settlement locations per security, we find ourselves incurring more and more exceptions just on the trade enrichment processing before we even get to the real problems.

Furthermore, the Operations area now needs to increasingly look forward at projected depo positions, much as Treasury have to do with cash. Now that the same security can appear in multiple depos, there is a need for real-time stock ladders to facilitate timely and accurate management of depo realignments. It follows that in order to have accurate projected positions, you must have an agreed starting balance on which to base the forecast, so daily stock reconciliations become essential. Once the starting depo balances have been agreed, the projected positions need to be monitored real-time as settlement confirmations come in throughout the day – the projections will change continuously as the current and previous days' open trades settle down. Because of the number of depos involved, it is not efficient to monitor them all for possible realignments. A projected short position does not necessarily mean that realignment is required; it is quite likely caused by a failed trade and therefore is not appropriate for realignment. The system therefore needs to be able to provide an exception-based enquiry focusing specifically on those securities with multiple depo balances, forecast or actual, which need to be assessed. Taking it a step further, the system could generate 'proposed' realignments, which the settlements area can then approve or reject depending on the information they have on associated pending trades.

The important thing to note is that the proliferation of exchanges with their cross-depository settlement relationships is conspiring against the fully automated STP environment the industry is striving for. On the one hand, the European Securities Forum (ESF) is pushing for ultimately one or, at most, two European CSDs while at the same time the new trading platforms are effectively increasing the number we already have by encouraging settlement of the same security in multiple locations. We assume things have to get worse before they get better!

Client service

With the growing trend towards cheap execution-only services, it has become increasingly difficult for broker/dealers to differentiate themselves from their competitors. Conversely, the fund managers, having driven their broker/dealers down to the wire on commissions, have looked at other ways of extracting greater value from their broker/dealers and, as a result, interest has shifted very much to the post-execution phase of the trade life cycle. Fund managers are now looking at the downstream costs incurred in their trading relationships and this has required broker/dealers to make settlement efficiency an intrinsic part of the overall product offering. In many cases settlement efficiency is the sole differentiating factor between broker/dealers, and the fund managers have been quick to take advantage of this situation.

Suddenly fund managers' Operations departments have found themselves very much in the driving seat when managing broker relationships. Apart from the demands made in the area of automated confirmation mentioned earlier, they have also found they can demand other value-added services from broker/dealers who are only too willing to provide additional services in order to differentiate themselves from the competition. Fund managers have taken the opportunity to receive even more information back from their broker/dealers in computer-readable form so that they can further improve their overall efficiency levels and risk management.

It is not uncommon for fund managers to request daily or even real-time pending trade reports from their broker/dealers to give them a more informed picture of the true status of the transaction. Used in conjunction with their custodians' pending trade reports, a view of the broker/dealers' transaction details will make for a much speedier resolution of settlement discrepancies. In many cases it will obviate the need for a phone call to the broker at all and, where it is still necessary, will facilitate a much more efficient conversation with both sides being able at least to see the broker/dealers' view of the situation.

This puts a whole new requirement on the broker/dealers' Operations systems in that they need to be web enabled to make the information available to their clients – fund managers do not want a bespoke interface for each broker they deal with. However, while the web provides a common delivery medium, the format and content will vary by fund manager so broker/dealers are increasingly having to develop tailored web-delivered reporting capabilities for their key clients. A lack of standards is making this very onerous for Operations and IT departments who can find themselves rolling out several new bespoke reports each week as clients become more demanding.

If the challenge of producing a multitude of bespoke reports is not bad enough, the underlying ramifications are even more far-reaching. Once you start making your system records directly available to your clients you open up a whole new set of issues, which strike at the very heart of systems architectures. As basic as it sounds, the most critical factor in this is security and client confidentiality. The technical level of security to prevent hackers is, hopefully, already in place and so will be employed to control client access to your extranet in the same way as any other external access is controlled. But there is now an additional level of security needed to ensure clients can see only their own data and not yours or that of other clients. Furthermore, they will have up to several hundred underlying funds on which they will want consolidated reporting. This demands additional levels of system security to ensure each client sees only their own accounts, which in turn requires these relationships to be defined in the reference data. If the reports are created automatically based on the static data, the chances are you will want to enhance both the manual and system validation around the set-up of these account hierarchies. If one of these links is wrong you could easily end up divulging one of your client's business activity to their competitor which will almost certainly result in the loss of both clients! If your systems are less sophisticated and the reports have to be hard coded with the client's accounts, then you have a worse control problem. This then falls outside the main operations control environment and into the world of user acceptance testing and system release control – not something you want to resort to every time a new client goes on-stream.

Going forward, we are likely to see broker/dealers giving secure access directly into their core systems as an alternative to the proliferation of bespoke reports. Apart from a technology challenge to ensure security and confidentiality, it raises a considerable number of broader business issues which need to be addressed before opening up your internal systems to clients. Because the client is looking directly at your core operational systems, any errors or delays in processing are going to be immediately obvious. If a clerk settles a trade incorrectly, or miscodes a status, there is a chance that the client will be looking at the system at that moment and take away incorrect information. Normally such errors are only transitory and are corrected before client-specific reports are prepared; now every wrinkle in your processing is on full view to the client. In addition, they will see every system stoppage and processing delay so unless you can be 100% confident of your internal operating standards you should think very carefully before opening up your systems and procedures to your clients whose confidence will quickly be lost with just a few bad experiences.

Exception-based processing

Earlier we talked about how high STP environments make the vast bulk of the business invisible to the Operations department which can result in problems also being hidden. In a manual environment, everybody has their set tasks allocated, to be carried out sequentially according to various deadlines, and the necessary controls are in place to make sure these get done – the procedures followed are reasonably routine and fairly consistent day to day. A manual process will generally have the following characteristics:

- Composed of a predefined set of tasks
- Tasks carried out sequentially to a set timetable
- It is routine
- It is predictable

In a STP environment the procedure for handling exceptions is neither sequential nor predictable. Exceptions occur on a random basis and will invariably be of a unique nature. A STP exception-handling process will have the following very different characteristics:

- Tasks are likely to be ill defined
- Tasks will need to be carried out at random to a changing timetable
- It is unpredictable
- It is chaotic

We therefore require a new processing model to manage and control what has basically changed from a well-ordered sequential process to a chaotic random one where tasks themselves are ill defined and invariably unique. Not only do we need a new processing model but it is also obvious that we need a much higher calibre of staff who can cope in this much more chaotic environment.

Again the industry is looking to technology to help bring-order and discipline to the area of exception processing by automating the exception-handling process itself. The key problems we face in managing exception processing are:

- Monitoring their occurrence
- Allocating exceptions to the most appropriate person
- Prioritizing them according to constantly changing circumstances
- Tracking progress and completion
- Escalating failings

What we are looking at is a Workflow solution, which will capture the tasks, assign them and track their completion.

Workflow solutions have been used in the manufacturing and retail industries for many years, typically handling orders, stock picking, packaging, invoicing, etc., but until recently have not made any inroads into the wholesale banking sector. Why this is so we are not quite sure but we would imagine it is because these industries have always worked with more static, prescriptive procedures which can readily be defined in a Workflow solution. So why, we hear you ask, are we suggesting a Workflow solution for exception handling which we have just described as a chaotic and unpredictable process? The answer is that while the exceptions themselves are random and unique in nature, the STP infrastructure imposes a very prescriptive procedure on the overall transaction chain. The automation of STP ensures tasks are carried out consistently and uniformly and so therefore we do know where exceptions may occur and we also know where they have to be returned once fixed. What Workflow will do for us is to look after the processing which falls out of the STP flow and return it back to the flow at the earliest possible point. This overcomes the problem mentioned earlier regarding the danger of things being missed in a STP environment.

In a Workflow environment, rather than have a predefined daily task list, Operations staff will, putting it very simply, sit around waiting to be assigned an exceptional task by the Workflow engine (Figure 1.8). The Workflow engine will pick up the exception as it falls out of the STP flow, decide who is the best group to deal with it and then allocate it to an individual within that group according to workload

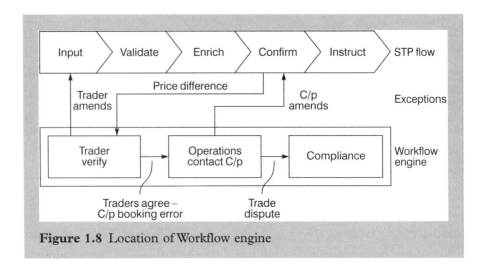

Figure 1.8 Location of Workflow engine

and priority. If it can't be fixed by that individual, it will follow an escalation path until it reaches someone who can fix it. As soon as it is fixed, the transaction is automatically injected back into the main STP flow to continue its journey.

Staffing considerations

This STP Workflow-based environment is going to radically affect the way Operations staff have traditionally worked and some may not be able to adapt. Exception processing-based environments will require more specialized staff with strong analytical and problem-solving skills. STP operations will have no requirement for the routine tasks of paper pushing, transaction enrichment and checking found in most of today's back offices. Staff in a true STP environment will, as we have already seen, deal exclusively with exceptional items which will require an analytical mind and specialist knowledge of the subject matter. All the routine tasks will be fully automated leaving only problematical tasks, which would today typically be handled by Supervisors and Managers. While a high STP environment will require significantly fewer people, the people it does require will need to be more, rather than less, highly skilled. This in turn will lead to much flatter structures than we are currently used to and will eliminate the traditional supervisor, manager career path to which Operations staff aspire. We will need to find new ways of managing and motivating staff in the brave new world of STP. It will undoubtedly be a higher-pressure environment in which to work, as the workload will be unpredictable, volatile, complex and deadline driven. Getting staff to adapt to the new world of exception processing will be as big a challenge as the implementation of STP itself.

Looking ahead, Operations staff will have to possess a much better knowledge and understanding of how the systems work otherwise they won't understand the process at all. With virtually all the routine tasks embedded in complex computer systems, there is nothing tangible left for people to relate to. Most people learn things by actually doing them so a clerk who has been doing a job for 12 months will generally be more expert than one who has only been doing it for one month. How will people learn or understand procedures they have never done? Now this is a conundrum – on the one hand, we need people to be more technically able in order to deal with complex exceptions and, on the other, we have a situation where it will be more difficult for those same people to obtain this knowledge in the first place! We suggest we will need to rely more on formal classroom education going forward as opposed to today's informal on-the-job style training.

In addition to the changing nature of today's tasks, such highly automated environments will require new skills within the Operations function to manage it effectively. We know only too well how tightly interwoven IT and Operations have become already and as we move closer to true STP the relationship is set to become even closer. If we consider that all routine tasks will have necessarily been computerized in our STP engine, then it is obvious that any and every change in business procedure will require a change to our STP engine. This is rather disconcerting because today, when we can still change many of our manual procedures without IT involvement, we still have huge backlogs of system changes awaiting IT resource and while we're waiting, we normally employ a 'work-around'. By definition, 'work-arounds' cannot exist in a true STP regime so does this mean our business will come to a halt due to the IT logjam? We don't know the answer to this issue but it would seem that Operations will require significantly more IT capability than it does now if the business is to be kept running. Whether this means Operations staff becoming more IT able or IT staff becoming more Operationally aware, it is difficult to say. Does it not also imply that we will simply replace Operations' clerical staff with more expensive IT staff to cope with the increased dependency on IT, a STP environment would seem to create?

Internal pressures

Control

The introduction of real-time settlement and shorter settlement cycles is creating a much faster, more dynamic settlement environment for Operations departments to cope with. Add to this the relatively high level of staff turnover in the industry and, in many markets, a shortage of skilled labour, you can see why firms are focusing increasingly on the control of their settlement processes. There have been too many instances in the past where controls have been absent altogether or have been vested solely in one person who, for whatever reason, has chosen not to react to what they are telling them. Controls should not be an 'add-on'; they should be an inherent part of the combined manual and systematized processes that are applied in the course of carrying out those processes, i.e. if the control isn't performed, the process comes to a halt and alarm bells ring as a result.

While systems are often accused of being inflexible, and by their nature they probably should be, they are very good at imposing procedures and enforcing control points. This is what we meant by controls being inherent in the tasks needing to be carried out to achieve the end result; the system will not allow you to continue until the necessary control checks have been completed. Not only do systems enforce this regime, payment instruction authorization being a good example, but they have the benefit of providing an absolute audit trail of exactly who did what and when. Any control not effected will cause a halt or delay in the process which, with adequate monitoring tools discussed earlier, will immediately escalate the failure. Although in practice there is a need for both, your primary controls must be preventive rather than detective; it's no good being alerted to a fraudulent payment the following day!

Automated controls have the benefit of being demonstrable on an historic basis to internal/external auditors and regulators which manual controls don't. These people also feel confident in knowing that control is not vested in a single point of failure and that digressions from the norm will be alerted to a broad management audience automatically.

The problem will be exacerbated further with the increasing trend towards 24-hour trading (and settlement) when it will no longer be possible to rely on the traditional end of day/start of day manual control checks. Controls will need to become proactive to ensure errors are detected and prevented rather than being detected after the event.

Reference data

Reference data is fundamental to STP and yet it has been largely ignored compared with the amount of attention the transaction life cycle has received. A joint TowerGroup, Reuters and Capco industry survey carried out in the latter half of 2001 found the average number of staff in each organization dedicated to maintaining static data was

58 with 10% of respondents having more than 200 assigned to this task. In spite of this huge expense, 79% of respondents strongly agreed that inaccurate reference data was the major cause of STP exceptions. Clearly this is an area that that will need to be addressed if we are to achieve the levels of STP necessary for T+1 settlement.

It is not only STP that is impacted by poor-quality reference data. Bad reference data can lead to more serious problems like outright settlement failure, incorrect accrued interest, mispriced valuations, to mention a few. It is ironic that we go to great lengths to automatically default transaction attributes and yet the source of the defaulting data is itself manually maintained and often recognized as being sub-standard. As mentioned earlier, while manual processes create sporadic isolated errors, automated processes generate large clusters of errors. High STP in the transaction-processing chain can take a single isolated error in the reference data and propagate it through all the downstream systems including profit and loss, risk management, position management, etc. A further cause of error in reference data is mismapping and misinterpretation of data fields between systems. It is quite common for multiple silos of reference data to be held alongside particular applications which use a unique method to store and represent their reference data. If this copy of reference data is maintained manually, operators have to learn new data structures and coding standards, giving rise to further errors on top of those already naturally inherent in any duplicate keying process. Where the data structures and representations themselves are different, judgements have to be made when transposing corporate data fields to cater for differences in both format and coding values. This only serves to make the static data maintenance function unnecessarily complex and introduce further inconsistency and ambiguity in the interpretation and use of reference data throughout the organization.

There will be increasing pressure not only to reduce the cost of reference data but also to improve its reliability as a key step towards true STP. This will necessitate the centralization of corporate reference data to reduce the cost of duplication and the implementation of corporate wide data definitions to facilitate seamless re-use of data across systems and functions. Ideally industry-wide data definitions to support inter-enterprise synchronization of data formats and meanings are needed and this is what SWIFT on behalf of the International Standards Organization has set out to do with the implementation of the ISO 15022 Data Field Dictionary (DFD) standard. The ultimate aim of the DFD is to provide an industrywide definition of all data items used in the processing of financial transactions. It covers data item naming, value representation and syntax and, just like a language dictionary, will ensure everybody has the same understanding of financial terminology wherever it is used. By using data items from the DFD to construct messages, which can be registered in the ISO 15022 catalogue of financial messages, anyone using such messages can effectively look up the individual data items in the DFD and be sure of getting the correct meaning. For example, '98A::TRAD//yyyymmdd' is how the business term 'Trade date' is represented in the ISO 15022 syntax and how it would appear in any messages adhering to this standard. There can therefore be no ambiguity in its interpretation wherever and however it is being used. Whether it is being generated by a fund manager in the USA or a custodian in China, the DFD will ensure both parties use and interpret '98A::TRAD//yyyymmdd' in exactly the same way.

It is worth pointing out at this stage that SWIFT fulfils two independent functions in this area. They are appointed by the International Standards Organization as the Registration Authority for the 15022 Securities – Scheme for Messages, message standard and have responsibility for maintaining the DFD and message catalogue. This includes issuing new data fields to the DFD and approving new message types into the message catalogue. Quite independently (Chinese walls) they provide the FIN and SWIFTNET networks for the secure communication of ISO 7775 and 15022-compliant messages. You should be aware, however, that the ISO 15022 securities messaging standard is in the public domain and can be used over other networks providing a similar level of resilience and security.

Corporate actions

Corporate actions departments are the least automated areas of a modern Operations department and yet they incur enormous peaks of activity during dividend seasons and year-ends, have to work to tight deadlines and carry huge risks. While the income-processing side (dividends and coupons) has been automated, the unstructured and complex nature of the corporate actions processing has kept this an almost entirely manual process. As a result the demand for corporate actions people is always high and consequently so is the cost – a prime candidate for a technology solution so why hasn't it happened?

First, corporate actions are at the bottom of the Operations food chain, relying on timely and accurate transaction processing and depo management data on which to calculate entitlements. It was therefore not possible to automate the asset-servicing functions until the upstream processing reached a minimum level of systematization to provide the necessary computerized records on which asset-servicing automation could be constructed. Second, many corporate action events are too complex to fit a fixed-format message structure so they are communicated in free-format text fields, which render them unsuitable for electronic interpretation. In addition, those data fields that can be structured are provided in a proprietary format by the data vendors requiring extensive and complex mapping to internal standardized formats before they can be processed. Similarly, the agent banks are encumbered with the same problems of event complexity and, with the old SWIFT standard ISO 7775, were very restricted in how much corporate action data they could communicate in a structured form. ISO 15022 will go a long way to addressing this problem. The result is a function that is over-sensitive to seasonal corporate action spikes in activity, increasing risk and producing mountains of paper!

The move to more proprietary trading activities has seen much greater plays on and around corporate events. Trading profit and loss on many of these complex trading structures is entirely dependent on the correct interpretation, election and execution of the event terms putting an enormous burden on the corporate actions area. Often traders will delay their decision right to the last moment as they monitor which way the markets are moving before electing, thus putting even more pressure on an already stressed process. Because the margins are small, the positions involved are necessarily large and so an incorrect or missed election on an event can give rise to massive losses. On the fund management side, the increased use of index tracker funds has brought more attention to the corporate action's function as the fund's performance is almost totally dependent on the accurate and timely collection of income and rights. Once fund performance is affected, so are bonuses and suddenly corporate actions have begun to receive much more attention from the front office. The stock-lending business has also contributed to increased risk in corporate actions by putting more dependency on the accuracy of data vendor feeds for notification of events. Where positions have been lent out, the depo positions may be flat and the agent bank will generate no notification, making you totally dependent on vendor feeds to capture corporate announcements.

The key areas for automation are the capture and verification of event data feeds and the workflow management of the event from announcement to collection. The foundation of good corporate actions processing is event data. Unfortunately, because of the extent and diversity of corporate events there is no one single provider who can provide 100% coverage of all events for all instruments across all markets, although some will claim to come close to this. Furthermore, none of the data vendors will guarantee the accuracy or completeness of the data they do provide. This means organizations have to take in several feeds from different vendors, and sometimes directly from stock exchanges or depositories, and compare event information across multiple feeds in an effort to substantiate its accuracy. This comparison process is proving difficult to automate because of the proprietary structures, formats and coding values used by the various vendors and as a result, much of this work is still carried out manually. Even where it has been automated, comparisons are not necessarily conclusive. Typically data sources will be evaluated on a simple voting basis; if three are the same and one is different, then the three will be considered to be correct. While this sounds logical, it may not necessarily be the case as it is possible that all three vendors picked up the same incorrect information. As a consequence it is necessary to follow up any difference directly with the registrar or company to guarantee complete accuracy. A further refinement of this verification process is to include the agent banks' event notification details with the data vendor comparisons – agreement across all sources including the agent will provide a very high level of confidence indeed. The introduction of SWIFT ISO 15022 structured message formats in 2001 will enable agent announcements to be automatically compared with vendor feeds but it will require a huge mapping exercise between the proprietary data structures of the vendors and SWIFT ISO 15022. When embarking on this exercise it is a good opportunity to review your own internal corporate action reference data structures which you may want to consider bringing into line with the SWIFT ISO 15022 DFD. If you do use the DFD, you will at least be consistent with the agent banks' field definitions in their notifications, as they will, of course, be using the ISO 15022 message types.

Following receipt of an event notification there follows a whole series of tasks, including calculation of entitlements, distribution of terms, reconciliations, execution, etc. all of which have to be done to a precise, and sometimes lengthy, timetable. Any failure along the way can cause incorrect election or missed deadlines, potentially resulting in significant trading losses. Traditionally these event processing calendars are set up in people's personal diaries which makes any sort of monitoring or automated escalation of impending deadlines impossible to implement. We are now seeing a trend towards automated centralized diarization of event timetables, which provides for supervisor monitoring, reallocation of events for workload balancing and automatic escalation of late tasks. It can also be extended to a full-blown workflow system with automatic distribution of announcements and entitlements to traders/fund managers, capture of elections, generation of execution notices and entitlement booking. This will provide a much more rigorous control infrastructure for what is now one of the highest risk areas in Operations.

Summary

We have looked at the drivers that have brought us to where we are today and touched on a few of the current drivers that are pushing our demands on technology to even greater levels of complexity and cost. In the following chapter we will examine how much IT can really do for Operations and, conversely, what it can't do.

Chapter 2

What IT can deliver

Introduction

Technology, although inextricably embodied in the modern securities administration environment, is not a panacea and does not absolve Operations of their responsibilities and duties. Technology will, when employed correctly, improve operational efficiency and quality but will never replace the need for highly skilled and experienced Operations management and staff. It is a key tool, but by no means the only tool which Operations have at their disposal to assist with the running of the post-execution transaction life cycle. It is also an increasingly expensive tool which needs to be used with great ingenuity if you are to reap the maximum benefit from the investment.

The use of technology has followed an evolutionary path with it initially being used in the automation of routine, high-volume tasks such as in the production of confirmations and settlement instructions as discussed earlier. These well-defined, well-proven tasks were comparatively simple to automate and with the consequential direct and immediate cost savings, Operations and IT were credited with some impressive successes. Because they were well-defined, routine processes, IT estimates for cost and time were generally fairly accurate and projects could be embarked upon with a high degree of certainty of success. In many ways both departments were riding the crest of a wave and thought that these quick wins could be achieved throughout Operations, reducing costs even further. Many people, especially those outside Operations, could even see the day when Operations would become a fully automated production-line environment with a limited number of machine operators overseeing the production line. This vision led to very large sums of money being invested in IT systems throughout the industry but to varying degrees of success. As the more complex, less routine functions were targeted for automation, project costing and timescales became far less reliable, requirements were more difficult to define and savings were less tangible. Even the projects considered to be successful rarely delivered to their original potential. Often large areas of functionality were missed or de-scoped before implementation. As a result (or maybe an excuse), users could, or would, not realize the staff savings originally projected in the cost – benefit analysis, thus throwing the viability of the project into question – unfortunately by this time it was too late as the investment had already been made. On top of this, the additional ongoing IT support costs, particularly in the days immediately after implementation, would almost certainly cancel out the already much-reduced user savings that could be realized.

There is a great incentive on both sides to automate as many functions as possible. Operations can see a problem being automated out of existence and IT see a chance to demonstrate their prowess with the latest technology. As you move closer and closer to a true STP environment, the case for further automation becomes increasingly difficult to assess as the risk of failure is greater and the benefits become less concrete. Do not automatically assume an IT solution is necessary – there is far more risk in developing an IT solution than in defining robust manual procedures. Before launching into an IT development you should be very clear on exactly what the problem is you're trying to overcome and what the ultimate objective is. Above all, do not think that technology solutions absolve Operations of their responsibilities. As a service provider to the business, Operations are equally culpable for a failed technology project as they are for a failure in their own procedural duties. Technology plays such a big part in the delivery of operational services, its efficient and effective deployment has become a key part of Operations management's responsibilities. Efficient use of technology will deliver an improved service, poor use will waste money and deliver a poorer service so to the end client it is all part of the one service (Figure 2.1). For example, if the point of sales terminals at your local supermarket were running slow and you had been queuing for over an hour to check out your basket, you would hold the manager of the store to account rather than the company's IT department!

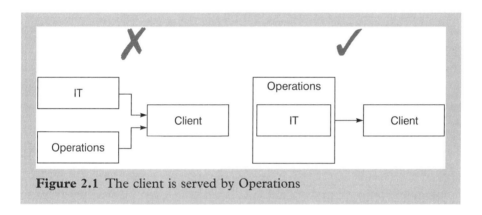

Figure 2.1 The client is served by Operations

This section goes through the questions that should be asked by both Operations and IT in respect of any operational problems that are being considered for a technology solution which will help to ensure that technology is used in the most effective way.

Understand the manual process

It sounds fundamental but so often Operations put forward proposals to IT, particularly where new business lines are concerned, before they have fully understood the business flows and processes themselves. Not only does this waste time but it loses Operations credibility in the eyes of IT and rightly so. If a new business line or product is involved then it is quite likely that it is not well understood and it certainly won't be well proven. Whereever possible get new business lines running on manual procedures which can quickly and easily be changed until they are firmly bedded down. This gives everyone a chance to fully appreciate the practical side of the processing requirements, learn from their mistakes and have a much clearer understanding of what the crux of the problem is and what they hope to achieve through the use of technology. Once you have a sound understanding of the process and the problem, you can then approach IT, clear in what you want to achieve, with less chance of being persuaded to compromise your requirement simply to suit the system. If you embark on these discussions without a very firm idea of what you need, you may find yourself being sold something much less suitable. In the absence of a concise business requirement's definition, IT will define the requirement for you which is likely to be influenced more by existing system constraints than the practicalities of doing the job in the real world.

In the initial analysis, do not confine your attention to the immediate problem. It may be that something upstream of your process is making life more difficult than it need be for no reason other than lack of awareness. It is normally much easier and cheaper to fix a problem at source than to build in allowances, manual or automatic, further down the chain.

Similarly you should be looking downstream to see what impact your changes might have further along the transaction life cycle. Again, it may be that by doing something a certain way you greatly improve someone else's lot for no additional cost or inconvenience to yourself. Figure 2.2 shows a very simple example of how we unnecessarily

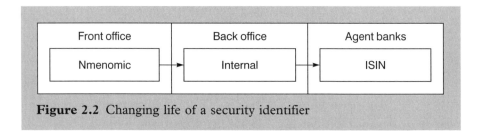

Figure 2.2 Changing life of a security identifier

complicate things for each other by using different codes to identify the same security.

Where old processes are concerned, be prepared to question them before initiating expensive IT feasibility studies. Manual procedures have a nasty habit of retaining functions that have long since become redundant and only serve to confuse and unnecessarily complicate the analysis and design process. Make sure that every aspect of the procedure has a purpose and fulfils an objective to avoid wasting scarce and expensive IT resource.

Optimize and rationalize the manual process

This is not about cutting IT out of the loop, it is about making sure the users have a practical understanding of how their business operates. This understanding is based around the business functions that need to be carried out to fulfil a business objective, some of which may already be automated and others still manual. At this stage it doesn't matter whether a function is computerized or carried out manually. The issue is whether a given function fulfils a business purpose and if so, it is being done in the right way in the right place and time. As systems evolve over many years, it is quite common for them to acquire and retain functions whose purpose has long since expired and are simply confusing the current business-processing model. What is worse is that they will absorb valuable resources every time the system is enhanced as they will also have to be maintained and tested, even though they have no business use, to ensure no adverse effect on the functions that are serving a purpose. It is essential that this analysis and understanding is based around business needs only, taking no account of technical implementations, and therefore is best carried out by the users alone. Users should be given some basic training in process flow analysis and documentation to ensure they produce the definition in a clear and consistent format. A good starting point for this exercise is desk-operating procedures. These won't provide the depth of detail required for the full analysis but they will supply the outer framework in which to work. If there are existing procedures, make sure they are still reflective of the day-to-day working practices – it is not unheard of for procedures to get out of date!

Following completion of the rationalization and optimization work, test the newly modelled process by implementing it through the desk procedures. You will immediately gain efficiency in the existing manual process from the use of the optimized procedure and will have a solid foundation on which to investigate the possible application of technology solutions. You may even find that your problems have been solved or, at least, alleviated without the need for a technology solution thus freeing up scarce IT resource for more essential tasks. Any misconceptions will be quickly highlighted through the use of the manual procedures and can be rectified accordingly – people are much more adaptable to change than software!

You can now approach the IT area, confident and knowledgeable in what you need to achieve, without all the baggage and confusion of irrelevancies. Not only does this do your credibility no end of good in the eyes of IT (not a bad thing), it will also save you a considerable amount of money by ensuring expensive IT resources are correctly focused from the outset. It will also prevent any undue influence, albeit well meaning, from IT on how you run your operation – it is very tempting for IT to tailor a user procedure to fit with the system model.

Is a technology solution appropriate?

Having now optimized your manual procedures and, with the necessary controls in place to ensure adherence to them, you can take a much more rational view of any proposals for IT solutions. IT resources are always limited and system request backlogs grow year on year. It is essential therefore that each need is carefully scrutinized if you are to avoid simply building up an ever-increasing wishlist of requirements. In this section we look at the questions we should be asking to help ensure that our requirement is deserving of scarce IT resource.

There can be a tendency these days to assume that any change in business requiring new or amended processing flows will immediately need to be reflected in additional or enhanced system functionality. This is particularly true in areas of already high automation where Operations' managers feel that any manual process will result in errors and that only an automated solution can guarantee risk free processing. First, this is not the right attitude of an Operations manager whose role is to ensure delivery of an efficient high-quality service. IT is not there to replace Operations, it is there to support them and make them more efficient but, at the end of the day, it is Operations who are responsible for service delivery. You should not be going down the technology route just to absolve you or your staff of their responsibilities. Second, IT quality is far from guaranteed and badly implemented solutions can cause the most disastrous results which will still be viewed as Operations short-comings by the business. Just imagine your personal banker informing you that it was the bank's IT group's fault that they incorrectly stopped that all-important payment – as far as you are concerned, it's time to find another bank!

It sounds strange but an adverse side-effect of increasing reliance on technology is that user staff begin to abdicate responsibility to their IT colleagues and see automation as an easy way out. How many times have you heard Operations staff claim they are ready but IT can't deliver the system until next year – it doesn't help the business at all! Operations managers should be clear in their responsibilities and, like any other manager, carry them out with limited resources.

Now that we have addressed the emotional issues, we should now question the commercial credentials of any proposed technology investment. Remember, we are considering making what is generally a significant investment on which we will require a competitive return over the subsequent 3–5 years depending on individual company accounting policies. So unless the business line has a longevity of at least a similar period, you are unlikely to receive the full benefit on your investment. Also consider the time to implementation of an IT solution. Even relatively minor changes will take several months at least, from initial conception to a well-bedded down, robust system. Many business opportunities these days are about exploiting niches in the marketplace with their maximum profitability coming in the early days before the competition catches up. These businesses need to be brought to market as quickly as possible and may have a very limited life span, becoming increasingly less profitable as time goes on. Under these circumstances an IT solution looks less attractive as its longer lead-time will preclude early entry to the market and its limited life-span will reduce the return on investment. IT is good at delivering solutions for strategic business lines, where you can take more time over the development and implementation to produce a robust platform that will give a return on investment over many years.

Another important consideration is the stability of the business and its associated processing requirements. Generally the initial period following product launch is full of change as people get to know the realities of running the business in the real world where things don't always go to plan. Processes have to be changed quickly to react to situations that had previously not been thought of to keep the product viable in terms of both client satisfaction and market competitiveness. This is not the same as understanding the processes discussed in a previous section; this is about the underlying business product itself changing in response to market forces and Operations having to adjust their procedures to suit. Premature automation of a dynamically changing business is not only wasteful of IT investment but can also be a constraint on the ability of Operations to react. It is much harder to work around an incorrect system solution than it is to adapt a manual procedure. As Operations managers you need to satisfy yourself that the underlying product is stable enough for you to invest in a more rigid processing platform.

Another popular argument to justify automation is transaction volume and, where there is significant volume that is perfectly reasonable. It is, however, one to be wary of, particularly in new business lines. Every business requires a critical level of activity and so there is a natural tendency for volumes to be, sometimes grossly, overstated at product-approval stage in order for it to demonstrate profitability. However, like any new business, in practice it can take much longer for volumes to grow than is forecast in the business plan so, while we wouldn't ignore volume predictions, we would certainly scrutinize them very carefully. Overstated volumes may delay implementation if they are so high Operations feel they cannot cope in a manual environment, while systems are developed to handle the overstated volumes. Furthermore, other projects will be delayed while IT resources are diverted to work on a project whose justification is less concrete. Unless it is blindingly obvious that volume will be an issue, consider agreeing some compromise transaction growth predictions and limits with the business and get it underway in a manual environment. It will soon become apparent how realistic the targets were and allow for a much more informed decision to be taken on the technology requirements.

Risk is another often-quoted reason for needing technology solutions and may very well be justified, but you need to be clear as to how and why the risk arises and how technology will mitigate it. Is it a complex process that Operations don't feel they can adequately manage? Risk normally arises out of complexity and the consequential increased likelihood of doing something wrong or not doing it at all. There are fundamentally two types of complexity, which have very different attributes and demand quite different approaches. Portfolio valuation and market risk models' complexity is in the derivation and proof of the underlying methodology and calculations. Once defined the model forms a relatively rigid, repetitive process albeit one which demands real-time, high-speed calculation of complex equations using continually changing market variables. This is simply not possible to do manually because of the sheer number of calculations and the speed at which they need to be carried out. This type of complexity is perfectly suited to, and can only be achieved through, the use of leading-edge technology. At the same time, it is not the sort of complexity we find in the Operations area. The complexity Operations has to cope with is concerned with the imperfections of working in the real world where human beings make mistakes, as opposed to the entirely predictable environment of a, albeit highly sophisticated, risk model program. Operations' procedures are rarely complex in terms of calculations or number of steps to be carried out. Their complexity comes about from having to achieve consistent results in an inconsistent and unpredictable environment – something even machines have not yet managed to do, at least in a commercial environment. It is therefore unlikely that automation will entirely mitigate the risk inherent in Operations' 'complex' operational processes because the processes are too dependent on unpredictable factors outside their control.

In summary, you are unlikely to come across a high-risk operational procedure whose risk can be significantly reduced through automation unless it is also associated with volume. In such a case, the risk would arise from not being able to carry out the procedure consistently with increasing volumes rather than not being able to carry out the procedure consistently in isolation – the latter is unlikely. Where you are justifying on grounds of risk, then you need to put some sort of measure on it so that you can see your starting level and your end level. Without going into great detail, risk is basically a function of likelihood of occurrence multiplied by the likely resultant loss, which must be given a financial value. It therefore immediately suggests that low-volume tasks, as you would expect, have a lower likelihood of failing than high-volume tasks. However, even if the likelihood of occurrence is quite high, the resulting losses may be very small and therefore sustainable. Conversely, failure in a very low-volume task may result in large losses, corporate actions being a good example where the smallest of errors in a complex process can result in massive losses. Technology will be able to mitigate your volume-related risk but its ability to assist with the process complexity-related risk is less certain which would explain why areas like Corporate Actions are among the least automated Operations functions in the industry.

Finally consider your specific problem in the bigger picture, not only within your own organization but also within the industry as a whole. Having gone through the above assessment process and having convinced yourself of a need for some systematization, look at what is going on around you. There may be other changes taking place that will have a direct impact on your immediate area of focus and so it may be more efficient to wait for these to come to fruition before rushing into your own systems developments that may require significant modification soon after implementation. It is perfectly reasonable to identify a requirement but put it on hold until the time is more relevant. It may mean some additional manual work in the interim but will be more efficient and less risky in the long term.

Will IT work?

We have now satisfied ourselves that an IT solution is necessary and we have agreed on the most appropriate timing for development and implementation. The only remaining question is whether it will work and to answer that, we first need to make sure we know what we mean by 'work'! We have talked a lot about understanding the business, the process and the rationale for a technology solution but all that this achieves is to make certain we know how to automate whatever it is we need to automate. We haven't so far defined the end objective and so cannot answer the question 'Will IT work?'. It may well work in as much as we have a computer doing what was previously done manually but what business goal has that fulfilled? Many projects are undertaken without a clear definition of the benefits automation is supposed to bring and are then held up as being extremely successful because they work in the sense of executing and following a defined procedure. The fact that there are the same number of people employed to monitor hitherto non-existent exception queues and that there is an additional IT support cost and that the client still receives his confirmations late somehow gets lost in the euphoria of implementing a mechanical piece of software. There are too many 'successful' systems implementations that fail miserably to meet any real commercial objective.

The business, or commercial, objective of any project must be clearly stated and agreed up-front as this is the basis on which we can determine whether it has 'worked' or not. This requires a step back from the workings of the process itself and must be defined independently of it—it is very easy for the objectives to be adversely diluted by giving too much regard to the means of how it is to be achieved. This objective should remain at the forefront of people's minds throughout the project and it is this against which the success or otherwise of the project is assessed. In fact it will normally be a very concise definition with no room for gradations of success – the objective is either met or it isn't.

This is particularly important for those projects sold on grounds of increased efficiency where there seems to be a law which states that original full-time equivalent (FTE) savings will tend to zero as the project nears implementation. Often the justification for not achiev-ing the target savings is de-scoping of functionality or functionality not being delivered in a user-efficient form. These are all valid arguments but at the end of the day, if the investment cost has been incurred and no, or only much reduced, savings are forthcoming, then the project has 'not worked'. If there is any deviation from course on forecast savings, they must be raised as soon as the first scope change occurs and, if necessary, the objectives should be revised and the justification reassessed. Too often the overall effect of functional reductions or deficiencies on the original goals are not flagged until just before implementation when it is too late to take any remedial action. Operations are responsible for delivering the ongoing savings so it is their responsibility to review all scope changes and functional requirements against this ultimate objective and shout very loudly the minute it is put in doubt.

Sometimes a technology solution may be justified on grounds of 'better control'. In this case we should be clear what is out of control and the cost of being 'out of control'. Very few Operations managers will admit to being out of control but they often want systems to give them 'better control'. It is also sometimes used to avoid having to cost-justify a project – 'we won't save anything but it will improve controls!'. It may well improve control but how will this improvement manifest itself in the bottom line? Perhaps it means the outstanding cash breaks come down by 50% or we incur 25% fewer interest claims as a result. On the face of it these figures sound very impressive but delivering a reduction in statistics may be of little commercial advantage. What's the point of reducing cash breaks by 50% if we only average a handful at present? It may be a very costly way of removing a few breaks off our key performance indicators (KPIs). Similarly on the interest claim reduction, if we are incurring only a few thousand GBP per annum in claims then a 25% reduction is insignificant. Controls are a means to an end, so when selling an investment cost based on improvements in control, not an unworthy aim, you must look through the control mechanism to the costs being incurred in the underlying business process due to failures in the execution of that process. In the first example we are interested in how much will be saved on overdraft interest as a result of having more accurate cash forecasting due to fewer breaks being outstanding. In the second example, we want to know how much less will be paid out in interest claims because the 'improved controls' ensure settlement instructions always go out on time. Control of processes is a means to an end, not an end in themselves.

There is considerable momentum to throw technology at operational issues in the belief that it will cure all ills and make for a quieter and cheaper life for those of us in Operations. There can't be an Operations group in the world that doesn't have at least several years' backlog of systems projects and enhancements, whose total forecast savings probably exceed the entire Operations budget, meaning that if they could all be implemented, you would actually run at a profit! This is clearly not possible so it pays to scrutinize each technology investment bearing this in mind because there are quite clearly a lot of proposals overstating their true cost effectiveness.

In summary, Operations managers need to get best value for money out of IT projects and ensure that they achieve a competitive rate of return on their investment. With the possible exception of regulatory driven technology investments, there must always be a bottom-line saving which will pay a return on investment. This saving must be stated and agreed by all parties up-front and kept firmly in mind throughout the project life cycle when evaluating scope changes and/ or cost overruns. Whenever there is a change in circumstances during the development life cycle, the main question you need to ask is 'how will it affect the original business objective?' In fact we would go as far to say that it is worth obtaining confirmation that the original objectives are still achievable at every project meeting if for no other reason than to keep it firmly planted in everyone's mind.

Beware the downside

Like any commercial investment there is always a risk that things may not go quite to plan. When embarking on, what you have shown to be, an apparently attractive investment, you must play devil's advocate and look at all the peripheral things that could have an adverse effect on the progress and ultimate success of the project. You cannot assume that because you have a watertight cost–benefit case success will be guaranteed. There are many other factors, some quite removed from the immediate vicinity of the project itself, that will conspire to delay progress, divert attention, increase costs, etc. which need to be taken into account when approving an IT initiative. Many of these factors will be beyond your control so it is essential to get them clear up-front so that the risks can be properly evaluated and an informed decision taken on whether they are manageable or not. We will now go on to look at some of these more remote factors that may have a bearing on the success or otherwise of a particular project.

Effect of project lead times

It is an unfortunate fact of life that even the most clear-cut technology initiatives have a habit of sitting on a priority list for many months before getting started. During this time much can change and what was a clear-cut case 3 months ago may not be so obviously attractive now. For example, some end-of-year processing enhancements look attractive a few months before the year-end, assuming a short project-elapsed time, but they will have a completely different appeal if trying to start them just before the year-end. You may as well wait until a few months before the next year-end and work on something that will give more immediate benefit. This is an obvious example but there are many other functions, which have seasonal usage, and are therefore best developed in synch with their season.

It is not just the lead-time to commencement of development but also the lead-time to implementation that has a bearing on a project's viability. During any significant IT development, Operations will be expected to commit a considerable amount of resource to the project which will take their most experienced staff away from the day-to-day running of the department. There's never a good time to second staff to projects but there are plenty of bad times which you would wish to avoid at all cost. Perhaps there has been significant staff turnover, which has left the desk overstretched just with their day-to-day work without having to take on project work as well. Alternatively it may be that there is another initiative that demands senior management focus and you wouldn't want another project to detract attention from it. In summary, Operations must be sure that build timing is right so that they can afford it the appropriate levels of resources and attention throughout the development life cycle. The implementation date must also be carefully scheduled to get immediate benefit but at the same time avoid clashes with other events.

Changes in the business and operating environments

Cost justifications will be based on agreed assumptions about the future internal and external business environment. However, the securities industry is infamous for its volatility and what is good business today might be unprofitable tomorrow. Investor sentiment can change extraordinarily quickly causing large falls in transaction volume literally overnight. Even in periods of relative stability, regulatory and tax changes can again have an enormous impact on particular business lines, although one would generally receive more advanced warning in this instance. Nevertheless, it pays to question the business on a product's robustness because the front and back offices have such different payback periods for technology investments. Front-office developments tend to take the form of rapidly developed tactical solutions to exploit a fleeting business opportunity whereas back-office developments have to be strategic and take account of all the other corporate requirements. This makes development of the latter much more cumbersome and less well suited to supporting short-term tactical business lines. In fact trying to systematize something with a limited life span, or at least an uncertain one, can have a negative effect on the business as it serves as a distraction to supporting it in a manual capacity.

It is not only the business that will have an impact on the effectiveness of Operations' technology investments. Operations must also consider the environment in which they operate and assess their investments in the context of an increasingly changing clearing and settlement infrastructure. For example, at the current time (2002) there is considerable upheaval in the European settlement arena, making it very difficult to assess technology investments. Your systems may be struggling with volume but do you upgrade for more capacity when there is the likelihood of going to central counterparty and net settlement? In the USA, where they have run a continuous net settlement (CNS) system since the late 1970s, they have seen netting efficiency levels as high as 97% in value terms which has, to a large extent, alleviated any volume-related problems as well as providing a significant reduction in risk. Your business case for increased volume capacity would look very different taking into account the effects of a CNS model.

Because of the much longer payback period on back-office systems developments, you need to satisfy yourself as far as possible that the business and operating environment will remain stable enough for you to recoup your investment.

Project risk

Two projects of similar size and projected return on investment may have completely different risk profiles. Generally systems which are self-contained will be of lower risk than those which entail many external interfaces. With a self-contained system, everything is within the control of the immediate project team who can change and adapt things at will to simplify their processing needs. Once you start dealing with external interfaces, you no longer have total control over your own destiny. You will have to cope with the nuances of interfaced systems and hence the level of complexity will naturally increase in line with the number and size of external interactions. Human interfaces are particularly complex to deal with because of the unpredictable nature of human responses and the necessity for the system to cope with, and stay in control of, the huge diversity of responses it is likely to receive. As a rule of thumb the greater the number of external interactions, human or system, the greater will be the complexity of the technology solution. Similarly the larger the deployed user base and geographical dispersion, the greater will be the complexity of implementation due to basic things like varying skill levels, language difficulties and coordination across time zones.

While this shouldn't be an overriding consideration, given two projects with equal cost justification, it makes good commercial sense to prioritize the lower risk of the two and therefore improve your chances of success.

Staff considerations

However well you do your homework, you will be doomed to failure unless you have the buy-in and commitment of your key staff. This can be a highly sensitive matter particularly if staff savings are part of the equation. There should not be any problem with the manager of the affected area because he will already be involved with the IT initiative and is more than likely its proposer. As part of the cost–benefit analysis he will already have a view of how his department will be structured to realize the savings following implementation. The issue is what do you tell the rest of the team, some of who will lose their jobs, and still ensure their continued support and commitment? There is no right answer to this question and managers will need to take account of their own circumstances and staff characteristics. However, our personal opinion is to be very open and respect people's professionalism and loyalty, although in this industry the latter is not something that is actively encouraged! You cannot hide the fact that a project is underway and it will be pretty obvious from what is being automated if jobs are going to be affected. We would recommend that from the outset, this fact is announced to the affected areas but without giving specific numbers which, in all fairness, one really cannot be certain of in the initial stages of development. As stated earlier, though, the senior management and project sponsors will be absolutely clear on what the target savings are but, as there is no certainty in projects, it would be unfair to disclose this absolute to those whose jobs may be part of that number. In a worse-case scenario it could be that the savings have been grossly overstated and while it is perfectly reasonable for the manager to be held culpable for such an oversight, you wouldn't want to worry the staff unnecessarily with a number that is fundamentally flawed.

Having recommended an open approach to staff savings, you must at the same time ensure that you are protected from any adverse reaction from them. Management needs to be extra vigilant at this time to ensure the continued smooth running of the department and needs to have key people secured in case of any staff backlash. In reality, most people are very conscientious and professional and if they feel they're being treated as such, they are more likely to accept the inevitable. If staff feel they are being deliberately excluded and they see clandestine meetings taking place between senior management, their hackles will be raised and their commitment lost. In this case the project is going to struggle from the outset as it is these same people who will need to supply the Business Analysts (BAs) with the fine detail and nuances of how their functions operate in the imperfect world of reality.

Apart from general staff morale concerns, you also need to consider whether you have the right staff on the desk who can work with IT to produce a sound systems requirements definition. Users with a good logical mind and an IT vision will make a considerable difference to the speed of development and quality of delivery. You need people who will volunteer information to the BA rather than wait for him to ask, people who will scrutinize and challenge specifications and, above all, people who are enthusiastic about the success of the project. Having worked in both IT and Operations, we have always felt it is easier for users to learn some basic analysis techniques than it is for IT to learn the business practises. Where as you can read plenty of textbooks about the properties and behaviour of a particular instrument, no such clear definition exists for administering its settlement. By providing a few high-calibre users with some basic systems analysis skills, you will close the knowledge gap between IT and Operations and help to ensure that those quirky procedures known only to the clerks on the desk are brought out sooner rather than later.

The hidden costs

By hidden costs we mean those additional ongoing costs that will be incurred as a result of computerization. They should have been factored into the cost–benefit analysis but sometimes get overlooked or substantially understated so we raise them here as a reminder. Each organization will have its own recharging mechanism, which you need to understand to ensure that costs are correctly recognized and fairly attributed. We will therefore talk about them in a generic sense, and while it may be that in your organization they don't show up, they do still exist and should be taken into account when justifying automation on efficiency grounds.

You will be amazed how many system software and associated licenses are involved in today's world of open systems and, because they are normally licensed by server or number of users, they form a considerable part of development and ongoing running costs. As an example, if your new application requires its own hardware server then you are potentially looking at an operating system licence, a database management system licence and any number of other software licences required by the systems infrastructure including security, communication buses, software release management, etc.

These licences typically have a purchase cost, which will be part of the capital expenditure of the project, but they also have an ongoing maintenance charge of around 15%–20% of the purchase price. This is to cover software bug fixes, technical support and version upgrades. Even where your organization has a site licence for a particular piece of software, you will find yourself picking up a proportion of the site licence cost in respect of your usage of it.

If you are buying packaged application software then there will, of course, be ongoing maintenance charges for your chosen application. In a distributed systems environment these may be levied on a server basis or by user or by a combination of both. User licensing may be further categorized by functionality so that, for example, those requiring update access cost more than those needing only read access. The licensing costs can be particularly prohibitive where an application is used by a large number of users infrequently or for short periods at a time. For example, cash and security reconciliation systems are used by the reconciliation's desk throughout the day, every day, but also need to be accessed by the rest of Operations on an occasional basis for short periods of time to investigate problems. In these cases, software vendors will often suggest a licence structure based on the number of concurrent users thus enabling any number of people to use the application but only so many at any one time, on the basis that no one uses it for very long. In practice these licensing structures can be impractical, as you tend to find even occasional users need to use the system at similar times and it gets very frustrating when you can't get logged on when you need to. As if this wasn't bad enough, you'll also be charged for licences on testing environments and disaster recovery platforms although with some work and negotiation it should be possible to combine these together.

We have talked about third-party software licensing costs but there are also the internal IT support costs of which you will find yourself having to take a share. These can be broadly categorized into two areas, indirect and direct. Indirect costs relate to general infrastructure charges that anyone using IT resources will need to take a share of. Typical examples of these costs are networking, database administration, desktop support, IT operations, Intranet, etc. These are infrastructure services that everyone uses to a greater or lesser extent depending on their requirements and are normally allocated on a simple per-user basis. Depending on the size of your particular project, you may just end up taking a small percentage of the total cost, reducing the recharge to other users. Alternatively, it may be of such a size that additional infrastructure support is required, in which case your particular application is likely to suffer the full marginal costs of providing it. In most cases the area concerned will already be using the corporate IT infrastructure and any increases should, at worst, be minor. However, should your application require infrastructure software different from your organization's standard operating environment, you will almost certainly be given a significantly higher infrastructure allocation. For example, if you acquire a package that requires a different database management system from your corporate standard, the database administration team may have to take on additional staff with the specialist technical skills needed to support it. In this case, as the only user of that particular technology, you will effectively end up paying for dedicated database administration rather than benefiting from the economy of scale of a corporate-wide service. This is unlikely to be cost effective in anything other than the largest applications where the large cost of this additional, dedicated infrastructure support can be absorbed.

The direct costs will depend on how much IT support your application requires to keep it running day to day and to maintain it in line with changes in the internal and external business environment. This is very difficult to estimate but a good starting point is to understand what the standstill cost will be assuming no enhancements will be required and all you need is the system to be kept running with bugs being fixed where necessary. Depending on the budgeting process, you will then need to estimate with IT how much enhancement work you think you will require over the period so that you can get a complete picture of your total ongoing support costs. In the months immediately following implementation you should assume there will be quite a high number of bugs that need fixing and functional modifications arising from its use by a much broader and diverse set of users. One would expect the number of software changes to fall as the application beds itself down, but these ongoing support costs can have a significant effect on the long-term viability of an application.

Apart from IT-related costs you should also be aware of additional user resource that will be required from time to time to carry out user acceptance testing for software upgrades, minor enhancements, bug fixes, etc. Generally you would expect this to be absorbed by the line but if you are thinly spread then you do need to consider whether you will be able to meet the demands of essential system support duties.

Used correctly IT will deliver

The preceding sections have focused on ensuring that an IT solution is really justifiable and that its objectives are achievable. It is quite negative towards technology solutions and this is deliberate. As mentioned earlier, there are already too many demands backlogged on IT work schedules that will never see the light of day so we do need to look much more probingly at technology initiatives to ensure correct prioritization of this ever-increasing backlog. So far we have considered all the pitfalls around selecting a badly conceived systems initiative and the questions we need to ask to ensure we stand a good chance of seeing a return on our investment.

There is no doubt that IT has brought and will continue to bring enormous benefits to the securities-processing business. However, it is a scarce resource and it is in everyone's interest to use it wisely. In this section we will look at the benefits that well-chosen systematization projects can bring to the Operations function.

Volume insensitivity

Although over the long term transaction volumes are growing at an ever-increasing rate, it is not a smooth curve and particular days or periods can be subject to large fluctuations above or below the overall trend. In addition, these sporadic spikes in volume have to be handled within the same fixed timeframe, to the same level of quality if settlement failure is to be avoided. By providing a straight through processing (STP) environment where only a small percentage of exceptions require human intervention, it is possible to manage such spikes without having to carry spare capacity. In a non-STP environment, the manual effort required is directly proportional to the volume. You don't get any increase in processing efficiency because each transaction requires the same amount of data enrichment and manipulation. In fact, processing efficiency will most likely fall due to the additional management and control overheads required to administer the increasing staff numbers, therefore a doubling of volume implies at least a doubling of staff.

In a STP environment, the impact of any volume increase is limited to the increase in the number of exceptions, which tend not to increase at the same rate as overall volumes. The reason for this is that multiple-transaction exceptions are generally caused by the same underlying problem – normally incorrect counterparty or instrument static data. When these problems are fixed, because transaction growth normally takes place within a similar universe of counterparts and instruments, the benefit of fixing the underlying static data once is leveraged by the additional volume which will be processed straight through. In a STP environment, the higher the volume, the greater the benefit gained from each problem fixed. Basically, most of transaction volume growth occurs within your core instruments and counterparts whereas exceptions will occur on the periphery of the core. You would therefore expect your effort to increase in line with the increase in exceptions which, as explained, will run at a lower rate than the overall growth.

Another aggravating factor is the spikiness of transaction volumes throughout a typical day (Figure 2.3). Generally the mornings will be fairly quiet with volume building towards the afternoon, reaching a peak at and around market close, making it very difficult to manage in a manual environment on an average day let alone a peak day. This is again where technology comes to our aid by insulating the Operations area from the intra-day volatility in trading volumes.

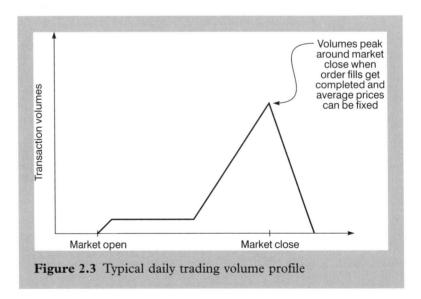

Figure 2.3 Typical daily trading volume profile

However, this condensing of daily trading volumes into a couple of hours around market close can cause problems for systems as well as users. When planning or evaluating transaction capacity, make sure you measure throughput per minute rather than throughput per day. Some vendors may quote what look to be acceptable capacity numbers but it assumes a nice even flow of transactions spread throughout the day. For example, a system may be quoted as being able to support 50 000 trades per day, assuming an even distribution of 5000 trades per hour. At first sight this sounds more than adequate for 20 000 trades per day but in fact runs into problems because 15 000 come in the last 2 hours. Securities-processing systems must be capable of handling large volumes in sporadic bursts rather than evenly spread over the course of the day.

While automation provides insulation from growing volumes and transaction peaks, you will need to be sure that volumes are forthcoming if you are going to achieve a respectable unit cost per transaction. STP systems are prohibitively expensive to develop and support and will cost the same whether they process 100 or 10 000 transactions, so the higher the volume, the cheaper the per-transaction cost. This is a dilemma facing small to medium-sized institutions who need STP to reduce, or at least stabilize, Operations costs but do not have sufficient volume to obtain an economic cost per trade out of the large technology investment needed to implement it in the first place. This will become a key driver towards outsourcing, especially as we near the introduction of even shorter settlement cycles.

Consistency

Technology is capable of delivering consistent levels of quality just not achievable in a high-volume manual environment. Furthermore, this level of consistency will be maintained through peaks in transaction volume and through periods of high staff turnover. This is becoming increasingly important as fund managers start to rate broker/dealers on the performance of their Operations service. Late confirmations with many of the larger fund managers will soon result in the broker/dealer being struck off the list of approved dealers irrespective of whether there was a peak in volumes or not. As firms cut costs, they have less capacity to handle hiccups in the daily activity so they demand consistent levels of service, day in and day out, from their counterparts regardless of volume levels. As systems and processes become more closely coupled across enterprises a delay in one organization will have a direct impact on the others so firms will increasingly want to deal only with firms who can provide a reliable and consistent quality service.

Staff flexibility

Technology forces you to carry out functions in the way the system has been designed to operate thus automatically enforcing a degree of standardization. There is far less scope for creative licence operating a system than when carrying out the same task manually and staff are naturally coerced into consistent practices themselves. These inherent standardized practises give the Operations manager much more flexibility when handling shifting workloads as staff using the same system will be working in a very similar manner even though they may be in completely different areas. Consistent procedures allow you to deploy a uniform set of control measures which, because they are developed only once, can be highly tuned to provide optimum control. Shortfalls in performance will be more apparent to senior management because they are looking at a consistent set of controls and will be more familiar with their interpretation than if they had to deal with a broader, more diverse set of controls.

Management information systems

Good management information is a vital tool for managing an efficient operation regardless of which business it is and securities processing is no exception. The key to good management information is correct and consistent interpretation of data to ensure that you are comparing apples with apples. Aside from the fact that it is extremely onerous to collect the necessary data in a manual environment and is last on people's list of priorities, it is also subject to misinterpretation. A very simple example of how people interpret things differently can be seen in transaction volume figures. In the case of a repo trade, a trader will see it as one transaction whereas the Operations department will view it as two! An equity salesman will count his agency trade as one whereas in fact there are two, one with the market and one with the client. By having all of your underlying data in a systematized form, it can be extracted and interpreted according to a centrally administered definition. Although not everyone may agree with it, it will at least guarantee consistency of use across the organization – a basic but important factor considering the size of decisions that will be taken on the basis of this information.

Kudos

The use of leading-edge technology carries a lot of kudos with clients, regulators and staff. The type of technology and the amount of investment in it is nearly always referred to in marketing material to woo prospective clients and employees. Large spending in technology is seen as a sign of your long-term commitment to the business and your clients, and will be considered a significant factor. Furthermore, if you are a highly automated organization, you will need your counterparts to have a similar level of sophistication if you are to obtain maximum benefit from your own technology and STP infrastructure. Systems work most effectively when interfaced to other systems, which ensures the necessary uniformity of information exchange required to achieve STP across organizations. An example that springs to mind is of writing out SWIFT instructions manually. While technically, the receiver doesn't know or care how it was produced by the sender, it will soon become abundantly clear when the system experiences the inconsistency of human nature and starts to generate exceptions all over the place. Lack of automation by your counterpart's can also backfire to disrupt the smooth running of your own operation. To take another example; you may have made an enormous investment in automating your settlement postings off the back of incoming SWIFT settlement confirmations to give you STP. Unfortunately, one of your agent banks produces his SWIFT confirmation messages manually to varying degrees of accuracy depending on volumes and staff absences! As a result of his lack of sophistication, the benefit of your STP investment is significantly reduced through no fault of your own. Where you intend to communicate with another organization electronically, the sophistication of their technology base will be a key differentiating factor in the selection process.

We spoke earlier of the difficulties the financial industry continues to have in attracting the right calibre staff and here again we see technology being used as a major attraction. Good-quality people don't want to write out hundreds of instructions day in day out, often requiring them to work late into the evening as well. They are far more likely to be attracted to an organization where the repetitive processes have been computerized leaving them to apply their skills dealing with the more challenging exceptional conditions. Staff also sees the use of high-tech systems as career enhancing particularly as many package systems are used by multiple organizations who will look for staff with specific systems experience and knowledge. This can, of course, also work against you.

Stability and control

Regulators also like to see good levels of automation as they see this as a sign of stability and control. We have already talked about how automation insulates you from the peaks in transaction volumes and staff turnover issues and this is seen as a good thing by regulators whose main objective is to oversee an efficient and stable market. There have been many instances of settlement backlogs building up due to firms' inability to cope with sudden and sustained increases in volume which can quickly lead to a shortage of liquidity and systemic failure. The ability to handle spiky transaction volumes is therefore a major factor in the wellbeing of the financial markets. Regulators also take a keen interest in staff turnover as they know that loss of knowledge and experience can lead to reductions in settlement efficiency which, again, can have adverse knock-on effects throughout the market. The more highly automated an organization is, the more knowledge it has tied up in its systems and the less susceptible it is to that knowledge walking out of the door.

So apart from the fundamental benefits in efficiency that high-tech quality systems bring, there are many side-benefits which are equally significant in running a stable, efficient Operations department.

What IT can't deliver

Finally we thought it would be interesting to conclude this chapter on what IT can't deliver to Operations – yes there are some things, believe it or not! With the increasing reliance on technology in the Operations world, IT has become a convenient whipping boy when things go wrong and there has been a disconcerting move to abdication of responsibility by some Operations management. Most worrying is a tacit acceptance that errors cannot be prevented in a manual environment and that when a manual procedure breaks down, it must be IT's fault for not automating it! Similarly people will insist that better system validation would have prevented an error or that the system should have alerted them to the fact there was something wrong. This is going too far and Operations must accept their responsibilities for service delivery to the end client. It is part of their responsibility to ensure that they receive similar high standards of service from their IT supplier and they must be clear that if IT fails, as far as the client is concerned, Operations fails. From a service delivery perspective the two are inseparable. Operations are accountable for service delivery and IT is just one of the weapons in their armoury to help them achieve it. Operations must employ a disciplined approach to the delivery of IT service just as they do for the delivery of clearing services. If IT are not performing it is Operation's responsibility to address it in order that they can do their job effectively and provide a quality service to the business.

Finally, although IT plays a key role in the overall Operations function, IT alone will not produce a quality Operations service. It is only by first having a quality Operations function that technology will be used to best effect. A poor-quality Operations function will not only deliver a sub-standard service, it will also waste money on ineffective technology investments.

Chapter 3

Working with technology – processes and information

Introduction

There is no doubt that technology is at the heart of the Operations function, but just how big a part it plays in the processes, procedures and controls can vary enormously. Some state-of-the-art systems can be found while some organizations still function, sometimes perfectly well, on some very old systems.

We have to consider the use of the available technology in relation to which part of the industry the organization operates in and also what kind of organization it is. The retail bank has a different structure, business and processes from an offshore fund and the need and use of technology is, of course, very different. Systems may be and are needed for a very large number of tasks, some critical and some less so. They are used for in-house purposes and as generators of products and services that are offered to clients. Systems are provided by external organizations or can be developed and maintained internally and all the time the entire business and financial markets industry is massively if not totally dependent on them.

So why and how are systems utilized?

Operations use of systems

If we consider the role of Operations we can see obvious ways in which technology is utilized. Record-keeping, calculations and valuations, communications to customers, instructions to agents, all require some element of computing power. Technology is used to receive data and then to produce data as Table 3.1 illustrates.

This is just a small example of the sources and uses of data and the Operations manager will need to have the full list of sources and data outputs to build comprehensive controls and procedures over the use of data.

Table 3.1 The use of technology to receive and produce data

Data source	Data output
Dealing system	Trade report
Exchange	Market/trade reconciliation report
	Prices and valuations
Clearing house	Positions and margin reports
	Matching and settlement data
	Settlement fails
Client	Contract notes/settlement advice
Custodian	Settlement requirements
Bank	Cash transfer instructions
	Cash book reconciliation
CSD	Asset reconciliation report
	Corporate action diary
SWIFT/payment systems	Cash movements
	Messages
Combined sources	Management information
	Statistics
	Performance measurement
	Static data

Some data is taken from a source and then used to produce reconciliation reports for other data from that source. For instance, positions and closing prices are taken from the exchange and clearing house and then the system utilizes that data in the production of position reports and reconciliation as well as margin calculations. In turn these are compared to other data from the clearing house, i.e. the margin calls as well as the data being then sent to other internal systems for production of, for instance, risk data.

This use and re-use of data is important as the credibility of the data is dependent on (a) the quality of the source and (b) any amendment of the data. We can see that for, say, derivatives business the critical reconciliation of the trader's position showing in the Operations system to the position at the clearing house in derivatives.

The credibility of the data is an issue from a systems point of view and also from the internal management point of view. If the data in the system is corrupted by program problems then any resultant problems can be blamed on the system. However, if the system has the right data but the Operations managers or others do not utilize the data, or use it incorrectly, then any resultant problems are not the system's fault. The famous exploits of one Nick Leeson is an example. The systems inside the organization had data on the exposure and positions that the company had but not all the data was being used in the reconciliation processes and critically important data on the positions from the exchange was only seen by Leeson. The result was that the true exposure was not seen until too late.

The use of data in processing is fundamental to the clearing and settlement process and Operations managers must ensure that the systems being used can actually provide the processing capability needed for the products and the volume of business. Key stages in the settlement process need different processing. If we assume that there are three phases in the clearing and settlement cycle then the use of technology at each stage can be identified.

Phase One: Pre-settlement

The use of data in this phase could include:

- Database
- Trade matching instructions
- Unmatched and error trades
- Asset and cash positions

Database

This is the driver for the system as it will contain the details of clients, products including international and internal identification numbers, contract specifications for exchange-traded derivatives including expiry data, settlement instructions, limits and data on corporate action dates and deadlines. This kind of static data can cause unnecessary delays and errors if it is not maintained correctly.

Trade matching instructions

On some markets where there is no central clearing counterparty process, the submission of trade matching instructions to the clearing house is required. Trade details are sent in standard formats to the clearing house for matching. Internally the trade data is either automatically generated from in-house dealing systems or is obtained from a deal or order ticket completed by the dealer and then input to the system by Operations.

This process can be allied to a confirmation process where the counterparties to the trade or the broker and client exchange confirmation of the trade details. Increasingly this is becoming an automated process as exchanges and clearing become electronic. Figure 3.1 illustrates the instruction matching process.

Unmatched and error trades

The ability to generate details of unmatched or errors on trades is vitally important. The longer an error remains, the greater the chance

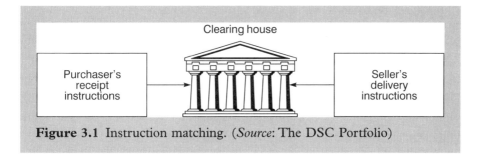

Figure 3.1 Instruction matching. (*Source*: The DSC Portfolio)

of financial loss but also, as settlement cycles in equities move towards T + 1, there is pressure for any problems to be immediately resolved. System-generated data on any unmatched trades needs to be seen by both Operations and dealers, dealers for resolution, Operations for asset and funding management, the unmatched deal possibly not settling on the original settlement date. Systems need to be able to help the Operations teams track the progress of any unmatched trade until resolution or deletion and to feed the data on these positions to the Operations manager and risk management (Figure 3.2).

Asset and cash positions

Without knowing whether there is sufficient asset or cash to settle trades on due date, an Operations team will undoubtedly have

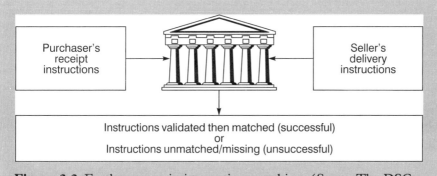

Figure 3.2 Further stages in instruction matching. (*Source*: The DSC Portfolio)

numerous problems and incur unnecessary losses. It is important that the systems can generate details of the assets held in safekeeping either internally or at an external CSD or custodian and also provide data on the amount of cash available for settlement. In both cases this will include actual and expected balances and the system will need to be available real-time so that changes to the asset and cash positioning are reflected as the trades settle and the cash flows in or out.

Phase two: settlement

As we move into the settlement phase itself the data being utilized will comprise:

- Asset/cash movement details
- Settlement instructions and messages
- Data on any unmatched transactions

It will be important for managers and supervisors to be able to track the progress of individual settlements so systems will need to be able to produce the necessary management information. This may include details of why a trade remains unmatched, what actions are being taken to rectify the situation and if the value is significant an escalation of the data to, say, the dealer and or risk managers.

Asset/cash movement details

The changes in the asset and cash positions need effective management and this requires systems to be able to provide up-to-the-minute data on the settled and unsettled items. The efficient placement or use of funds is also crucial and the person dealing with the positioning of assets and funds needs accurate and timely data. We need to have the data on the assets held based on available and unavailable assets. Unavailable assets will be those where we have lent the assets or they are currently being utilized as collateral and the data will need to show for how long these assets are unavailable so that other action can be considered should a settlement fall due.

The data on assets held and availability is provided to the dealers to enable them either to operate stock lending or advise operations on stock lending/borrowing if they are managing the process.

Settlement instructions and messages

Instructions and messages are increasingly automated, SWIFT messages being an example of the internationally available facilities used. SWIFT (The Society For Worldwide Interbank Financial Telecommunications) is a worldwide community of financial institutions whose purpose is to be the leader in communications solutions enabling interoperability between its members, their market infrastructures and their end-user communities. SWIFT utilizes message types and supports ten categories (Table 3.2).

Table 3.2 The ten categories supported by SWIFT

Category	Message group
0	General Information
1	Customer Transfers and Charges
2	Financial Institution Transfers
3	Financial Trading (FX, Loans, SWAPS etc.)
4	Collections and Cash Letters
5	Financial trading (Securities)
6	Precious Metals and Syndications
7	Documentary Credits and Guarantees
8	Travellers Cheques
9	Balance Reporting, Rate Changes, Nostro Statements and Status Enquiries

Within the message types there are many specifics covered. For example if we look at Category 5 – Securities Messages there are eight sections and within the eight sections there are some 70 MT500 series messages. The eight sections are:

1 Trading Instructions and Confirmations
2 Settlement Instructions and Confirmations
3 Corporate Actions and Event Notices
4 Capital and Income Advices
5 Statements
6 Securities Lending/Borrowing
7 Inter-Depository Clearing Systems
8 General

The success of SWIFT is due in small part to the growth in business in the markets and in particular the international business. As this cross-border activity grew, the use of paper and non-standard forms of communication hindered efficient settlement of transactions. Banks in particular had problems back in the 1960s and in the early 1970s a group of banks developed an automated telecommunications system with common standards. From this came SWIFT and today it operates in nearly 200 countries and for over 6000 institutions who communicate with each other 24 hours a day and send over 1 billion messages a year.

Cross-border securities processing is a complex business utilizing information and data from various sources including client, custodian and broker. Technology used by a firm has to be able to interface into this process so that vital instructions and information can be shared and problems resolved.

Data on unmatched trades

Unmatched trade data is vitally important. Any unmatched trade represents a risk of financial loss or ultimately even default by the counterparty. The operations team needs to be able to identify and report unmatched trades to both the operations manager and the dealers. The systems need to be designed to generate not only details of the unmatched trades but also length of time outstanding, cause, etc. As the unmatched trade may in turn affect a firm's ability to settle another trade, the data is vital to enable stock borrowing and even buy-ins if appropriate. Operations managers must be aware that data on unmatched trades needs to be built into procedures for controls and risk management in the Operations environment.

Processes in clearing and settlement

The processes in the clearing and settlement cycle can be broadly said to flow from the investment cycle illustrated in Figure 3.3. At every stage technology is likely to be heavily involved.

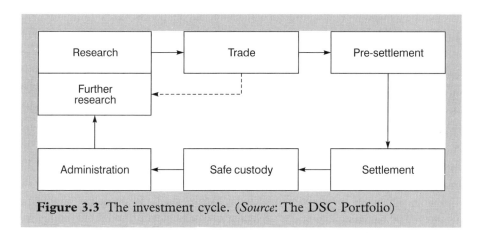

Figure 3.3 The investment cycle. (*Source*: The DSC Portfolio)

Various parties are, of course, involved in the process and utilize the technology in different ways. Custodians operate systems that provide for not only core activity but also the added-value services that clients need like securities lending, investment accounting and performance measurement. Clearing house systems must provide data about trades matching and settling, margin calls and, in the case of derivatives, exercise, tender and assignment for deliveries. Fund administrators systems must be able to receive the data about trades, record them in the fund and then revalue them to produce the Net Asset Valuation of the fund and prices for valuations of unit trusts, etc.

Custodians and fund administrators need to have systems able to deal with stock lending/borrowing and corporate actions and to

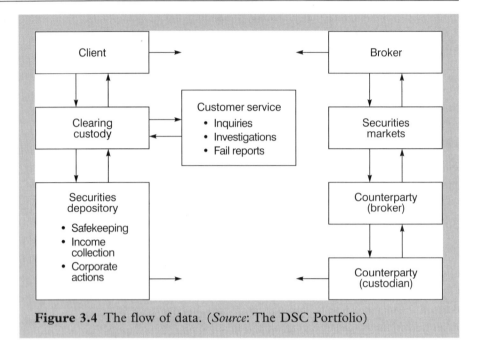

Figure 3.4 The flow of data. (*Source*: The DSC Portfolio)

produce any number of reports needed or requested by the clients and in some cases regulators.

Figure 3.4 further illustrates the flow of data. We can see from this figure that the processes generate information and instructions. Performance measurement to ensure that these processes are being carried out efficiently is very important not only for benchmarking by the client but also to the Operations managers to gauge how well the team is doing and where there are problems. This is achieved by relying on the systems to generate management information.

Management information

What management information does the operations manager need? Essentially it will cover areas such as:

- Settlement
- Safekeeping
- Reporting

- Client Services
- Cash Management
- Commissions and Fees
- Technology

Systems will provide data on such actions as:

- Percentage of trades settling on due date
- Failed trades by cause, product, counterparty etc.
- Incorrect instructions generated
- Market claims (in and out) for lost interest
- Corporate actions
- Dividend/Interest collection
- Reconciliation breaks
- Reporting timeliness and accuracy
- Client trades settled on time
- Problems and resolution rates/times
- Income/cost of funding and assets lending and borrowing
- Commissions received and fees paid
- System performance

The manager will utilize this and other information to produce several key pieces of information.

1 Cost of processing a trade
2 Settlement performance
3 Trends in business and in errors
4 Risk mapping

The use of systems to deliver this kind of information is central to the overall operations function and the information requested and the uses of that information can be diverse.

Summary

Working with IT is something that is vitally important to the ability of the operations manager to do their job. We have seen in this chapter just how much information and communication is at the heart of everything to do with the operations function. Operations managers need to be able to make the most of technology to support what they do, be it management information or processes or enabling operations to provide revenue generating added-value services to clients. The combination of quality technical managers and skilled, experienced operations managers is a very powerful one and potentially sets a firm apart from its competitors. To make it work, Operations managers need to be able to manage IT projects, understand budgeting and know what deliverables are realistically achievable given the operational and IT considerations. We look at this in the next chapter.

Chapter 4

Operations and IT working together

Introduction

So far we have looked at the industry developments that are driving the need for greater automation and the benefits, and new problems, a high-STP environment bring to the Operations function. We are now going to consider how we best put these various IT initiatives, some large, some small, into practice by taking a disciplined and rigorous approach to the management of IT service delivery. The chapter is structured into four main sections:

- Initiating an IT solution
- Managing IT developments
- Managing IT suppliers
- IT budgets

Initiating an IT solution focuses on the incubation of initiatives put forward for technology solutions and how we ensure only those with a solid business case make it onto the ever-increasing backlog of IT developments. Managing IT developments looks at how projects should be managed from the user perspective and in particular how users' tasks should be defined and progress monitored. There has been a tendency in the past to leave it all to IT but we have learnt from experience that the success of a project is as much dependent on the users as it is on the technicians. We then go on to consider the supply of IT services, whether they be internally or externally provided, and how they can be managed to provide the most cost-effective service. At the end of the day IT is another service provider to Operations which needs to be managed just as you have to manage your agent bank network. Finally we take a brief look at how to budget for IT services.

Initiating an IT solution

Today's Operations department is likely to have many tens of IT projects in progress at any one time with several years' backlog of outstanding requests vying for prioritization, most of which will never see the light of day. Demands for IT resources spring up all over the Operations function and every one, according to its originator, will be top priority. Furthermore, what was high priority last week has this week been superseded by an 'urgent' priority and so it goes on with the priority list changing more frequently than the proverbial English weather. Unless this situation is properly controlled from the Operations side, IT will be bombarded with a never-ending stream of disparate requests, many of which will have not been properly thought through, all of which will be top priority. Their work programmes will be continually interrupted as they are diverted from one half-finished task to another in an attempt to comply with the continually changing priorities they are receiving. This results in many tasks being suspended in a half-finished state, loss of knowledge as people are moved off part-way through to another task, never to return to the same one and generally a dramatic drop in IT productivity.

In order to get the best from IT, Operations need to coordinate their system requirements across the whole department so that IT can be given a firm priority list of requirements to which both sides can dedicate their attention. This also ensures that the various initiatives are compatible with one another and any dependencies between them can be readily identified. Because there are so many demands for systems solutions, at any one time you need to be focused on a manageable subset that has concrete business benefits and buy-in from all parties. This way, people can channel their energies into a small core of initiatives that have agreed, clear cost–benefits rather than spreading their energy across the whole wishlist of requirements (see Figure 4.1).

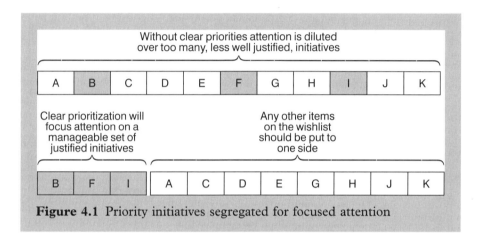

Figure 4.1 Priority initiatives segregated for focused attention

This section looks at how we go about coordinating the demands for IT resources and ensuring firm priorities are established to create a more stable and productive work programme.

Coordinating IT demands

Within Operations you need to establish a procedure around a central point through which all requests for IT services, or for that matter any changes, should be channelled. Depending on the size of the Operations department, this central point may be an individual or even a small team. The important thing is that the individual or group has a broad knowledge of the whole Operations area along with the systems employed so that they can help to identify areas of duplicated or conflicting initiatives. In a large organization, this function would ideally be staffed with a mixture of Operations and IT analysts who could simultaneously cover business and technical considerations.

The aim of the function is to provide an initial sifting of proposals by ensuring they:

- are clearly defined and well thought through
- have a concrete business case
- don't conflict or overlap with other initiatives
- are correctly prioritized

The resulting priority list can then be put before a joint business and administration steering committee to ensure it fits with the overall business and administration strategies (Figure 4.2).

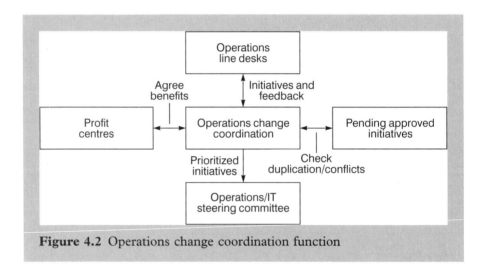

Figure 4.2 Operations change coordination function

Normally you would expect the steering committee to meet quarterly, setting priorities for the 3 months following the subsequent quarter. This prevents short-term changes in priorities and allows IT to plan and manage their work programmes more effectively. You should always aim to have a rolling frozen 3-month schedule that will only be changed in exceptional circumstances (Figure 4.3). This may seem an unnecessarily tedious and lengthy process but apart from enforcing good practice in the initiation stage it gives IT and Operations a very focused set of objectives to work on and prevents

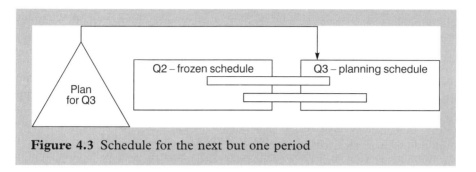

Figure 4.3 Schedule for the next but one period

disruption from changing priorities. How many times have you heard people blame late delivery of a task on changing priorities?

You will require some sort of system for capturing and processing the various initiatives arising throughout Operations so that a central list can be maintained. It is essential that the whole department can view this list so that they know what the current priorities are and what is on the agenda in the immediate term. Creating an awareness of pending changes will not only boost morale, it will elicit feedback from anyone in the department who may have a concern with a particular change that may have been overlooked.

Finally, it is important that anyone taking the trouble to propose an initiative receives constructive feedback, particularly if it is put as a low priority or rejected completely. Unless they get timely constructive feedback on their ideas, they will simply not bother to suggest any and the department will lose the benefit of their creativity.

Specify business objective

The most important thing to get across to Operations staff who are likely to be raising requests for system changes is to make them look at it in the context of its underlying business objective. So often, people will have good ideas on how to 'improve' something but it will only be for operating convenience or cosmetic appearance. While everybody should be actively encouraged to make proposals for system improvements we must be certain that the originators have a fully considered understanding of what it is they are trying to achieve and how it is going to benefit the organization. By this we basically mean how much cost it will save, how much existing revenue it will retain or how much new revenue it will generate. i.e what is the return on my investment? It comes back to what we talked about in Chapter 2 where we emphasized the importance of having the business objective clearly defined up-front so that the cost–benefit can be accurately assessed and everyone is clear on how success will be measured.

To encourage this discipline we have employed a standard template which must be completed before a proposal will even be considered by the IT coordination function. We have found that having to write down their proposal in a structured form forces people to think through their own ideas more thoroughly and can even result in them resolving their own problem without resorting to an IT solution. The use of a standard template also makes it easier for all interested parties to review and compare different proposals, particularly the Operations IT coordination function who will be evaluating initiatives across the board. Something else we have found useful is to make people assign their request to one of four discrete classifications, which not only assists the prioritization process but again focuses their mind on explaining the real underlying business objective. The categories we have found work quite well are:

- Regulatory/Industry
- Business constraint
- Risk
- Efficiency

We will now expand on each one of these as it is important to understand their definition and the supporting business case you would expect to accompany them.

Regulatory/industry

Where the change is required for regulatory reasons, one assumes that failure to implement the change will leave you in breach of regulation. Generally you would not expect to have much choice over requests in this category but even regulatory breaches need to be subject to a cost–benefit case. For example, if a new reporting rule or deadline is introduced then clearly, if you want to remain in that business line, you must comply otherwise risk losing an entire revenue stream – an unsustainable cost.

However, if a change is classified as regulatory because it will help to prevent occasional misreporting of, say Trade Reporting, this is not as absolute. A limited number of breaches in that particular area may be acceptable to the regulators and they would probably prefer you to invest in reducing your outstanding settlement backlog instead. Even so, a categorization of regulatory should certainly bring it to senior management's attention.

Changes in the industry-operating infrastructure can also leave you no option but to carry out the necessary enhancements to your systems to remain compatible. CSDs and ICSDs are continually upgrading their systems, as are agent banks, which require you to comply as long as you wish to remain in that market. The Euro and Y2K were two extreme examples of changes over which industry participants had no option but to spend large amounts of time and money in order to comply.

Business constraint

Without the change the business is being directly constrained and is either losing revenue or is being prevented from increasing revenue as a result. It could be that a product line that is currently being handled manually is to be expanded and without automation, the Operations area cannot support the increased volume. On the other hand, it could be that existing clients are demanding a quicker turnaround of their confirmations otherwise they are going to take business away. The first is a constraint on expansion while the latter is a constraint on the status quo. It is worth segregating requirements constraining the business because first, it is important that the front office is made aware of them and, second, they may consider sponsoring a solution from their own budgets, particularly in the case of new business lines.

Risk

Any change must be considered that will reduce the level of operational risk and the overall cost of current or projected operating losses. The reason for segregating these is that while the likelihood of the risk occurring is normally uncertain, the impact in some cases can be catastrophic. As much as anything, these types of changes need to be raised with senior management to make sure they at least have an awareness of them. The difficulty with risk-justified changes is how to quantify them so that a meaningful assessment and prioritization can be made. A very simple method we have seen used is to put the likelihood of occurrence into bands assigned a numeric value, do the same for likely loss and multiply the two together to give an overall risk factor which can be used as a guide in prioritization (Table 4.1). Additionally, for each risk you can plot the likelihood

Table 4.1 Frequency and impact ratings

Likely/actual frequency	Less than once per year	1
	Once per year	2
	Once per quarter	3
	Once per month	4
	Once per week	5
Likely/actual impact	Less than £10K	1
	Less than £100K	2
	Less than £1000K	3
	Less than £5000K	4
	£5000K and over	5

*Note: Risk factor = Likely/actual frequency *Likely/actual impact*

against the loss in a chart to give a clear visualization of relative risks and thus where you should focus your efforts. See Figure 4.4 for an example risk-ranking system.

A word of warning when calculating the impact, though; the estimated loss should be that which is incurred as a direct result of the operational error and it should not try to take a view on market and credit risk. As an example, if on a FX transaction you pay away funds to the wrong counterpart you have incurred full principal risk as there is a chance you may never get them back. Don't assume they would be paid away to a creditworthy institution and therefore would be returned with, at worst, the loss of a few days' interest. As far as Operations is concerned, the exposure is paying away funds to an incorrect counterpart, which incurs full principal risk. On the other hand, settling a DVP trade incorrectly can, at worst, give rise to risk of interest claims or protection of rights under a corporate event.

To aid visualization, each risk can be plotted on a chart to highlight those areas requiring priority attention (see Figure 4.4).

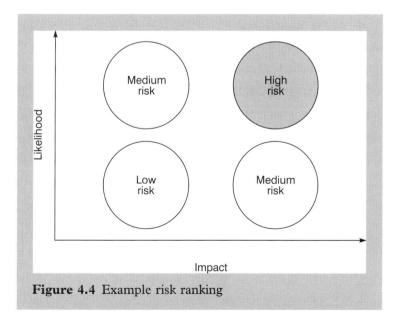

Figure 4.4 Example risk ranking

Efficiency

Generally this will be the biggest category and be the subject of most discussion as people fight for their particular cause. The business case should be on bottom-line savings, which in most cases will mean heads. We shouldn't, however, assume that all savings are necessarily desired even where there is a clear and quick payback. If it is an area supporting a low-volume, high-margin product line, the business may not be concerned about reducing the support head-count as the amount saved may be insignificant in the context of their business. They may well prefer to have the comfort of knowing there is spare capacity for a rainy day and are happy to pay the higher costs. This is why it is so important to get the underlying objective published from the outset to make sure all interested parties understand the motives for change. One thing to beware of when looking at efficiency improvements are cases based on fractional head-count savings. You obviously can't save half a person! In these cases there should be some other value-added service, **required by the business**, that the group will be able to perform as a result of the half a head saving. Alternatively you should look at packaging together enough small efficiency savings to sum to a full head saving. You will find that if you save half here, a third there and another third later, you never realize the whole head-count because the individual fractions just get lost. Whereas if you package them up, it is clear from the outset that the objective is to save 7/6 of a FTE and following implementation at least 6/6 can be immediately realized.

Basically any change request must be assigned one and only one classification. Where people argue that more than one is applicable they must chose the one which they consider carries the most significance. So, for example, if a system change is required for regulatory reasons but will also reduce costs, it must be classified under regulatory on the basis that a regulatory breach is more significant than a cost saving. Figure 4.5 shows a suggested template for proposing IT initiatives, which should help people to think their ideas through more thoroughly and present them in a more structured and consistent way.

System change request

Initiator:		Priority: ☐ High ☐ Medium ☐ Low
Change reason: ☐ Regulatory/industry ☐ Risk ☐ Business constraint ☐ Efficiency		

Problem description

- Describe the problem symptoms in business terms
- How/why is it affecting the business?
- Include business cost of not doing enhancement
- Use examples of costs incurred unnecessarily where possible

Business objective

- Describe objective in terms of impact it has on the business
- How will it directly benefit the business?
- Describe how the business will look after implementation
- Quantify the benefit against which the cost will be judged

Proposed change

- Describe in non-system terms what needs to be changed – maybe purely a change in manual procedure
- Do not describe how it is to be achieved – leave that to IT
- Include non-system-related operating changes, additional controls etc.

Potential risks

- How complex is it; what are the chances of success?
- Will attention/resources be diverted from other critical tasks?
- If something is being automated, what happens in the event of a systems failure?

Out of area impact

- Consider the effect this change will have on other areas – good or bad
- Will other areas need to make corresponding changes to systems/procedures?
- Could your change be simplified by another area making changes?

Figure 4.5 Example change initiation form

Finally, these change requests should be reviewed and prioritized by the IT coordination function and, where appropriate, put in front of the joint steering committee for preliminary approval. At this point it is also worth pencilling in a proposed sponsor and assigning an Operations owner who will be responsible for driving it through to implementation (Figure 4.6). The change request should be retained as the anchor point for the initiative as it progresses through the development life cycle to ensure the original business objectives are kept to the forefront of peoples' minds.

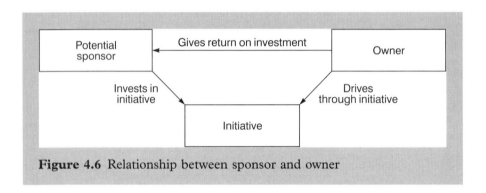

Figure 4.6 Relationship between sponsor and owner

Initial sizing

Once we are satisfied of a good business case for a systems solution, the first thing you need to know is how much it will cost so that we can be sure whether we still have a viable business case. At the same time, we do not want to spend a lot of time on a detailed feasibility study only to find the estimated cost far outstrips the benefit. What we need to do is to get a very rough order of magnitude of the project's size so that we can see whether the cost and benefit are in the same ballpark and hence whether it is worth scheduling a more detailed scoping exercise. This is where you need an experienced project manager, who knows your systems environment well and can quickly come up with a ballpark figure without diverting his project team from their work in progress. At this stage we are not looking for a figure to hold IT to, we just need to know whether it is worth scheduling a more detailed analysis which itself will start to incur costs and will need to be prioritized in with the rest of the work programme. In the past we have used three basic, highly imaginative categories; small, medium and large, roughly equating to less than £50 000, less than £500 000 and £500 000 or over respectively. It sounds too rough and ready but remember, we are only trying to make sure we eliminate the no-hopers before absorbing IT resources. Also, because it is a very superficial estimate it cannot be anything other than rough and ready but it is sufficient for our purposes at this stage.

As an example, one of the desks has asked for a new pending trade enquiry which they need for a specific market which they estimate will save them one Full Time Equivalent (FTE) or approximately £50 000 per year. However, the initial sizing puts the change in the 'large' category so even though the saving sounds very attractive in isolation, the return on investment will not be quick enough. Assuming the request was being sold on efficiency grounds then it would not be worth pursuing any further. One might argue that because of the limited investigative work that has been undertaken, the estimate could be wrong, and indeed it could. However, an experienced project manager is unlikely to be out by such a large factor that he assigns it to the wrong band particularly when you consider how broad they are. In addition to this preliminary costing, you would expect other macro issues that will have a bearing on the change request to be raised at the same time. For example, if we consider the example new enquiry change above, perhaps IT have plans for a new system upgrade which will incorporate this new requirement. So, even if the cost–benefit was attractive, you would almost certainly wait for the upgrade and get it for free rather than enhance an old system with a limited life expectancy.

Preliminary cost–benefit

Following the completion of the initial sizing exercise you will be able to present a preliminary cost–benefit. At a minimum this will either rule it out completely or keep it in the picture for further investigation and, at best, it will give you a feel for the strength of the business case which will have a bearing on its prioritization. If the initial scoping forecasts a payback within 12 months then that particular initiative should probably be given priority for detailed estimation as it sounds to have a solid business case. Where the initial sizing exercise has shown the benefit to be more marginal, you may take a decision at this stage not to proceed and concentrate on those initiatives whose benefit is more clear-cut and therefore stand more chance of succeeding.

At this stage the objective is very much on building confidence in the business case before committing valuable resources to it. Unfortunately there is no relationship between the user's perception of change size and the cost of technology required to implement it. We have all seen examples where the smallest change in the eyes of the user can have a massive impact on systems and occasionally we have seen it the other way round! This initial evaluation of system changes is there to stop us making such irrational assumptions and ensure that only changes which stand a fighting chance are invested in for further refinement and drilldown of their business case.

Preliminary prioritization

So far we have carried out a high-level cost–benefit analysis to ascertain whether the savings and the investment cost are in the same ballpark. For those that are, we now have to estimate and prioritize a detailed scoping and estimation study which will hopefully enable us to produce a more accurate and practical justification. We say hopefully because there is still the possibility that we may uncover something in the detailed investigation which completely overturns the view of the business case from the preliminary cost–benefit exercise.

Depending on the scale of the change, a scoping and estimation study can take a considerable amount of time and effort and therefore has to be scheduled into the IT work programme like any other piece of work. There is a tendency in the user community to assume that, given a three-line (including the heading) business requirement definition, IT can estimate the cost to within an accuracy of plus or minus £10 in their tea break! Unfortunately this is not the case and in reality providing detailed estimates is a time-consuming process which will distract IT resources from other commitments. This is why it needs to be prioritized and scheduled like any other piece of work to prevent IT's work programme being continually interrupted. It should take its place alongside other proposals with firm estimates for consideration of priority. Just because it is a scoping and estimation study doesn't mean it automatically jumps to the front of the queue ahead of the core developments. The joint steering committee should consider it on the merits of its preliminary business case and prioritize it accordingly. For example, if a particular initiative's preliminary business case has it paying back in 3 years then there is no point prioritizing its detailed estimation above changes which have firm business cases paying back in 1 year. In addition, there is far less certainty over the business case for the initiative which is being scheduled for estimation than there is for those which have already had their business cases refined and are scheduled for actual development.

We should also consider regulatory and client implications in addition to straight cost–benefit although if the cost–benefit is expressed correctly we should still be able to prioritize on the same basis. There may, for example, be circumstances whereby we have to make a change to satisfy regulatory requirements but it does not give us any savings or additional revenue and so these would naturally have to be prioritized according to their deadline rather than cost–benefit. Having said that, if you express the cost of not doing it in terms of shutting down the business, you will almost certainly have a very convincing cost–benefit case that will prioritize itself on that basis alone!

Scope and estimate

The objective here is to define and agree the content and boundaries of the change on which to base a more detailed estimate. Obviously the estimate is dependent on the scope definition so the exercise would normally be conducted in two parts with the estimate being worked out once agreement was reached on the scope. The scope will only define the core functionality that is to be provided and will not necessarily say how it will be delivered. Just as importantly, it should specify what isn't included so that the impact of the change can be clearly bounded not only within the overall systems environment but also within user functions.

As an example, let's assume the settlements area wish to have all pending trade statuses converted to a standardized internal format for ease of recognition. The scope will specify which statuses will be converted, which reports/enquiries they will appear on whether they can be used for searching etc. This is fine for the originators of the requirement but perhaps Treasury would also like to see the standardized codes and perhaps Client Services want to make them available to clients. You can immediately see how the impact of a relatively small change can start to spread, significantly altering the size of the task as it does so. We liken scope definitions to the ripples spreading out from a stone landing in a pond – if you don't contain them the ripples will eventually reach all the banks. You therefore need to put a ring around the entry point of the stone to limit the spread of the ripples. In the same way you can diagrammatically draw a boundary around the heart of the change enclosing those areas in scope and excluding those that are not to help visualize the scope.

Based on the above example and looking at the associated scope diagram in Figure 4.7, there are three points to note:

1 The notation is completely non-technical and makes no reference to systems components.
2 It shows very clearly that in this instance, CSD/ICSDs are out of scope as are Treasury enquiries and client reporting.
3 It makes no suggestion as to how the change will be achieved.

By avoiding any technical or system notation in the scope diagram we allow users to see the wood for the trees and avoid any

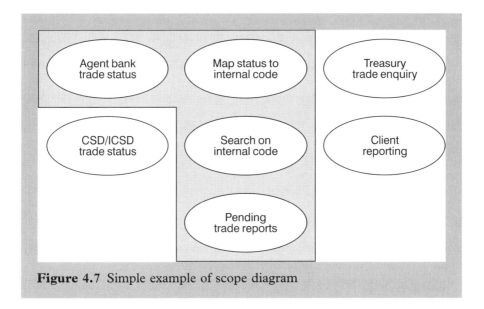

Figure 4.7 Simple example of scope diagram

misinterpretation of what a particular system component does. Restricting the notation to basic business terms, we ensure the users understand what is and what isn't in scope and leave IT to work out to which system components this will map.

Other key information required in a scope definition is transaction volumes, response times, numbers of users and amount of data as this **will** have a direct bearing on the technical solution and the cost. A system may be functionally perfect but if it can only handle half the required number of users then it will not achieve its objectives.

Don't think of this as purely an IT exercise. There will be user costs as well to consider including; additional staff to work on the project, technical training, possible redundancy payments, new procedures, etc. All these need to be factored into the estimate so that a total cost–benefit measure can be obtained.

One final note on how to handle the estimation of ill-defined or problematical areas of functionality which always seem to arise and delay completion of the scoping phase. First, it is important that the scoping phase itself is time bounded because it is one of those jobs that will otherwise expand to take up as much time as you let it. Second, remember this is an estimate not a quote, so where there are particularly fuzzy areas that cannot be bottomed out in the available time, do as the building trade does and put in an allowance to allow for the worst. This way, if the cost–benefit turns out to be so marginal that the allowance can tip it either way, it's probably not worth taking the chance. On the other hand, if the case is still solid with the allowance, then you can afford to go ahead even with a degree of uncertainty.

At this point in the process you should have sufficient information available to present a compelling business case which you can sell to the sponsor.

Sell the business case

We now have the concept, the benefits, a reasonably detailed estimate of costs and timescales and, assuming it adds up, all you have to do is sell it! It is much better to wait until you have all the facts and figures at your disposal before going on a sales campaign. You will be much more confident in your own mind and your case is more likely to stand up to scrutiny by prospective sponsors than if you go to them earlier. Furthermore, at this point Operations and IT are working in harmony so you will not get any contradictory messages from either side – there is nothing more damming than for the proposers to disagree among themselves when presenting the business case. You should also expand your audience at this stage to create awareness and generate more buy-in from other areas. Something the business feels it is marginal but is strongly supported by another area in the organization may tip the scales in your favour, although there is a chance it could also go the other way. The most important thing, though, is that you are being open with all interested parties and giving them the opportunity to have their say, which in itself suggests you must be pretty confident of what you're proposing. This raising of awareness and getting buy-in at this stage will be invaluable should the project run into difficulties later.

The two main points you need to get across are the underlying business objective and the risks. It is difficult for people to question savings and IT development costs because they won't have sufficient information available to them at the time. As we discussed earlier, the business will be interested in the underlying objective and how it aligns with their business strategy. You could be presenting a watertight case for reducing the traders' costs by $x\%$ year on year but if they are making stacks of money, $x\%$ on their bottom line may be immaterial to them. In fact they are probably more concerned with making sure the business they are winning is not disrupted as they stand to lose much more by losing business than they stand to gain from cost savings. In this situation they will be more interested in the project risk, and this is the other key issue you need to address. No one is going to feel too happy approving an initiative that carries a high probability of failure no matter how good the benefits appear. The failure of any project in itself is a bad thing but unfortunately projects do not tend to fail in isolation – they have a habit of dragging the current environment down with them. People will need to be convinced that the risk of failure is tolerable and that there are adequate contingency arrangements in place at least to maintain the status quo should things start to go awry. In fact, projects don't necessarily have to go wrong to disrupt day-to-day business. Secondment of experienced resources from the line and the additional management distraction can be enough to cause degradation in service levels. The business will want to be assured that there is enough strength in depth, in both the Operations and IT areas, to manage the additional workload successfully.

Decision to proceed

Based on feedback from presentations of the business case, and assuming majority support, the request should be put before the Operations/IT/business steering committee for final endorsement. This should be largely a rubber-stamp exercise as a general consensus on the wisdom of the initiative will have already been obtained. In the case of an initiative with very marginal benefit, then the steering committee may well find themselves making the final call or they may throw it back for further proving if they feel the objective is sound but the cost–benefit is uncertain. Similarly they may feel that an unacceptable level of risk is being run and ask for this to be mitigated further before giving approval.

At the same time as they approve it, the steering committee will assign it an appropriate priority relative to the other work programmes already scheduled. As we discussed earlier, you would expect it to be scheduled for the quarter three months hence but if they feel it is such a compelling case, they may prioritize it for scheduling in the immediate quarter.

Firm scheduling

Now comes the tricky task of scheduling the work in accordance with its relative priority. Unfortunately it is not a simple case of putting priority 1 ahead of priority 2, ahead of 3 etc. because there are many other factors to take into account. First, you must consider any externally imposed constraints which may influence the development and/or implementation target. Obvious examples include implementing year-end accounting changes just before rather than just after financial year-end, not implementing at the same time as another major change, trying to avoid heavy holiday periods etc. Once you have taken account of these absolutes, you then need to work within your own internal constraints.

One of the most difficult problems for IT is synchronizing availability of specialist technical skills with the timing of the tasks they need to carry out. This is further complicated by the complex network of dependencies that attach to most tasks in a project. So not only is it necessary to synchronize each task within resource availability windows, you must also ensure that all the preceding dependencies have been completed before its start can be scheduled. Fortunately this is part of the project manager's art but it is important to appreciate the complexity of putting a large schedule

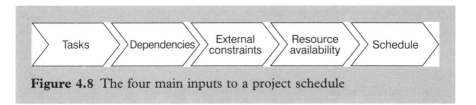

Figure 4.8 The four main inputs to a project schedule

together (Figure 4.8). We will talk about project plans in more detail in the next section.

Finally, once you have arrived at an agreed schedule you must, what is called in the trade, baseline it. This doesn't mean you cannot reschedule tasks in the light of progress but what it does mean is that anything you do reschedule will be clearly visible. You don't want to fall into the trap of having the schedule moved to stay in line with progress – if the project is behind, you want the schedule to show it.

Managing IT projects

Project management is all about delivering an objective to an agreed budget within an agreed timeframe. This section will not teach you how to be a project manager but it will hopefully give you some guidance on how to ensure, as the client, that the project is managed efficiently. You could liken it to having building work done at home. The builder would manage the project to see that all the separate trades were scheduled according to their interdependencies but you would want to be satisfied at regular intervals that things were going to plan in terms of both what was being constructed and the time it was taking. In fact, you would be more interested in how much longer it was going to take and we'll talk about this more later.

We have called this section 'Managing IT projects' but the principles apply equally to small enhancements although we would recommend combining smaller pieces of work into more of a 'project'-sized package to justify a project approach. First, you can apply a project management discipline without incurring what on a small task would be an uneconomic overhead and second, as mentioned earlier, you can combine fractional FTE savings to make whole FTEs to ensure that the projected savings can be realized. Also the term 'project' attracts more attention within the organization than 'enhancement' and attention is no bad thing to help focus the mind. You might say what gets watched, gets done and the more senior the watchers, the more likely it is to get done on time! Another problem we have found in working with small enhancements individually is that the focus on each one is diluted by however many are in progress at the same time. Taken individually, a missed deadline is no big deal, so you start to get lots of missed deadlines and cost overruns which cumulatively is a big deal but is not obviously apparent. What you need is a small enough subset of work programmes on the table at any one time to which everybody can give their full attention and ensure that they run according to plan.

The rest of this section is all about making sure that you, as the owner of the project, are aware of progress and are satisfied that things are progressing along the right path to meet the underlying business objective. Remember, even if the project is on schedule, if the deliverables are not in line with the business requirements, you won't be able to realize the savings on which it was originally justified and that is going to reflect on you.

Again, think of it in terms of a construction project at home. You wouldn't wait three months before looking at what the builder was doing. Even though you may not understand the technicalities of the individual stages of construction, you would be out there most days checking what you can see against the architect's drawings to make sure it is heading in the right direction. An IT project is no different in that you need to be able to see things along the way that you can relate to that will confirm how things are progressing to the end objective.

Critical success factors

Critical success factors go hand in hand with the underlying business objectives but focus instead on what key features must be delivered in order for the business objective to be achieved. They are not particularly scientific but are designed to give all parties in the build process a common focus on what needs to be achieved. In long, complex projects, it is too easy to get absorbed in the minute detail and drift away from the macro picture, so critical success factors are there to remind everyone, users and IT, of what must be achieved. In order to achieve this they need to have good punchy definitions and be few in number – even on a large project you wouldn't expect more than about ten. If you have too many, they start to become more diluted, less clear-cut and ultimately indistinguishable from the specification itself. Critical success factors are high-level definitions of key functions which, if not achieved, will prevent the business case from being realized. It is worth looking at an example to illustrate how you might arrive at them.

Let's say our business objective is, 'To reduce Operations head-count on the equity settlements desk by five by automating the sending of settlement instructions', a very clear and worthy business case. However, it doesn't give any sense of what has to be delivered in order for this to be achievable, particularly for the developers working on the project. It is too woolly to focus the mind when designing individual functional components because '. . . saving five heads . . .' is not something a computerized function can achieve. We need to express it in terms of the broad functions that will need to be provided to attain the ultimate goal. In this example, you would be looking at something like:

- 99% of all equity trades across all markets and trading platforms will have their settlement instruction generated with no manual intervention
- 100% of all equity trades will have their contingent accounting entries generated with no manual intervention

■ a central database of static data will be maintained to support the automatic defaulting of standard settlement instructions for 99% of all equity trades across all markets and trading platforms.

By specifying absolutes, it brings it home to people just exactly what is being demanded of them. In the above example, IT are going to be far more cautious about committing to 99% of equity trades being processed completely hands-off than they would be about the more fuzzy '. . . automated sending of settlement instructions'. By mentioning things like 'all markets', you will immediately alert the Business Analysts to the fact that each market may have its own peculiar nuances and therefore guard against only getting a partial automation which will not allow you to realize the associated savings. It is these critical success factors against which you will review and interpret project progress and any changes of direction.

User project management

In addition to the overall project management role, generally fulfilled by IT, there is a definite requirement for an Operations person to manage things from the user side. We would recommend assigning a user project manager to work alongside the IT project manager whose efforts will focus on coordinating and chasing the user tasks. User staff always seem to respond better to one of their own managers and he will similarly be more in tune with their problems and concerns. He will, of course, work in concert with the overall project manager to assign and schedule pieces of work according to their dependencies and staff availability. Although the user workload, at least in the early stages of the project, isn't as heavy as that of the developers, much of it will be on the critical path and will hold up large amounts of the work programme if it is not completed to schedule. Because much of this work requires the input of specialists with line responsibilities, there is a natural tendency for it to take second place after the day-to-day duties have been dealt with, consequently often resulting in it being delivered late. We will talk about monitoring progress a little later but we would like to emphasize now that user tasks need to be completed to schedule just as much as the developer's tasks and any slippage in this area will delay the project as much as any other. In fact, failure to complete user tasks to schedule will often have a greater impact on overall timescales because there will be many following tasks whose start time is dependent on their completion. In our experience, it is often the users who fail to meet their target dates in the early stages of the project but rather than have whole development teams stand idle, we press on regardless. This results in a significant watering down of user input, less rigorous sign-off of requirements and often, a lot of expensive and frustrating reworking further down the road. Users must recognize their obligations to projects and make the necessary commitment to make them happen.

Unless it is a particularly large project the user project management will not be a full-time role in itself but should be fulfilled by one of the senior, full-time user staff seconded to the project who will have specific tasks in addition to his project management duties. It is also important that the person in this role has a good network of contacts throughout the business. Nearly all projects will require some input from areas remote from the immediate vicinity of the project and a user with good relationships will be much more effective in coordinating these inter department activities than a technical project manager drafted in from outside, as is often the case. A good network within the organization is a tremendous advantage in getting things done at all, let alone on time!

Project plan

While the functional specifications define exactly what is to be built, the project plan defines exactly how it will be built and is equally important. There can be a tendency for the users to take the project plan with a pinch of salt and rely completely on IT to produce it and report progress against it without really having a view on it themselves. In this section we will look at the main features of a project plan that will enable you to understand and critique project schedules you will undoubtedly be presented with, normally by IT project managers.

The project plan needs to encompass all the pieces of work that need to be carried out, including those which will be undertaken by the users, so it is essential that the users take an active part in its creation and maintenance. Not only must it include project-related tasks, it must also include other events that may influence the project's progress. For example, there may be seasonal periods of high business activity where you don't want to implement system changes, there may be periods of staff shortages, such as the summer months, where you can't schedule user project tasks etc. All these tasks and events need to be reflected on a consolidated plan to ensure that, they are all taken account of in the scheduling process.

Another important aspect of the project plan, normally represented in the form of a Gantt chart, is to show dependencies between tasks; that is, Task B cannot start until Task A is completed. Many tasks will be able to proceed in parallel, their timing constrained only by resource availability, but there will be many others that must follow on sequentially because they rely on the output from a preceding task. It is the tasks that must be completed sequentially that have the greatest influence on the overall project completion date because no matter how many resources you throw at them, each one cannot start until its predecessor has finished. The sequence of such tasks is known as the 'critical path'. Any delay here will invariably delay the end date of the project because the lost time cannot be made up simply by throwing additional resources at it. In Figure 4.9 we can see that Tasks A and B can be done in parallel but Task C is dependent on Task A and Task D is dependent on Task C. From the schedule we can see that Tasks A, C and D are on the critical path and therefore determine the overall completion date of the project. We can also see that Task B has some slack in that as long as it is completed before Task D finishes, it will not impact the overall project end date. In this simple example we can immediately see that we need to give more

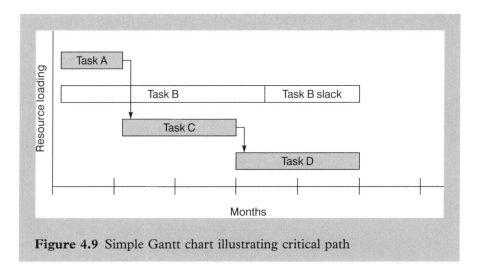

Figure 4.9 Simple Gantt chart illustrating critical path

management focus to Tasks A, C and D and if necessary move some resource from B to the tasks on the critical path as there is no advantage in finishing B way ahead of D.

In the preceding example, we have taken account of inter-task dependencies but we haven't considered the availability of the resources required to carry them out. So, not only do we need to identify the tasks, we also need to assign the appropriate resource to them and again, we will face constraints because only certain resources will have the requisite skills to carry out a given task. Continuing with the above example, we'll now assign some resources and see what this does to our schedule. To keep things simple, we'll assume we only have two resources X and Y. Figure 4.10 shows the resource loading following assignment of resources to their tasks.

We now have a problem in that Resource X is scheduled to carry out multiple tasks at the same time which, assuming they both require him or her full time, is not realistic. To start with, we cannot start Task B until after Resource X has finished Task A, so let's see what this does for the plan (Figure 4.11).

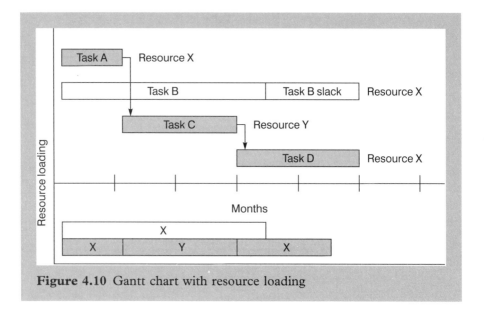

Figure 4.10 Gantt chart with resource loading

While we have solved the resourcing conflict between Tasks A and B, we have now exacerbated the conflict between Tasks B and D. By delaying Task B, it now overlaps even more with Task D which also requires resource X. You will also note we are rapidly losing the

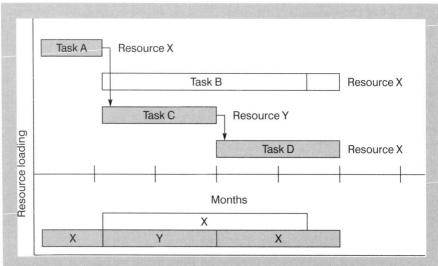

Figure 4.11 Gantt chart showing resource conflict between Tasks B and D

slack we had on Task B due to its start date being moved back. We now have a choice as to how we resolve this conflict. Option 1 would be to delay Task B until Task D has completed but this would lose us the advantage of X working on Task B while Y is working on Task C. It would also make Task B's start date dependent on Tasks A, C and D's end dates – any delay in either would delay the start of B. The second and best option, assuming tasks can't be split, would be to keep B where it is and delay the start of D. This way, although we still have to lengthen the overall project plan, we create some slack for Task C and by starting the longer of the two tasks (B and D) earlier, shorten the overall time to completion – see Figure 4.12.

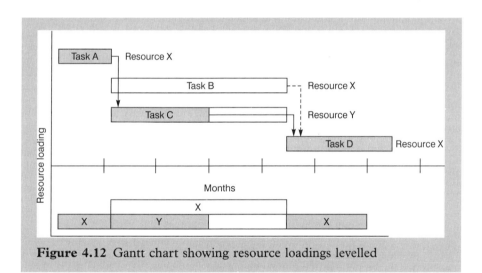

Figure 4.12 Gantt chart showing resource loadings levelled

In the figure you can see that as a result of resource constraints, we have had to extend the project end date by one and a half months and have added a resource dependency to the critical path. Although Task B is not on the critical path by nature of its content, because it requires the same resource as Task D which is on the critical path, it effectively becomes part of the critical path because any delay in Task B will delay the overall finish date. Having said that, you should not show it as such because you may decide to employ an additional resource that will allow Task B to be completed as originally scheduled in Figure 4.9. By contrast, although Tasks A and C are assigned different resources, Task C cannot start before Task A finishes because it requires Task A's deliverable as its input.

It is apparent that even with only a handful of tasks and resources you can quickly get into complex scheduling scenarios so on a typical project with hundreds of tasks and tens of resources, you can begin to see just how complex it is to get the optimum schedule.

Tasks and deliverables

We now want to look at the individual tasks on the project schedule and consider the level of detail they should go down to and how we know they have been completed. In the previous example we saw how even a few tasks can require some complex juggling of resources and tasks so it is important we don't create an unnecessary proliferation of detailed tasks that will render the job more complex than it already is. For managing the overall project individual tasks should be defined at a level where they produce tangible deliverables that can be signed off in isolation. For example, a data clean-up task may involve analysing the existing data, producing exception reports, gathering missing data, etc. but for the purposes of managing the overall project, we are only interested in knowing when the data clean-up in its entirety will be finished. Including too much detail will simply dilute the focus on the task as a whole as people become distracted in the low-level detail. We therefore look at the individual tasks and define them in terms of the deliverable they need to produce. To take the previous example of data clean-up, the deliverable needed is a clean set of data loaded into the production database because only then can we, for example, implement the new confirmations function which needs the additional data, captured as part of the clean-up exercise. Reflecting the completion of the individual steps does nothing for us in managing the big picture and, at worst, can actually cloud it.

Defining tasks in terms of their deliverables also gives you a concrete measure of their completion which is essential for accurate progress tracking, i.e. the task is not complete until you have the deliverable in your hands. This avoids the problem of the different interpretations people will have on what the task requires them to do which normally leans towards the least possible! This problem is actually most acute in the user community and is best illustrated by an example. Say we have a task 'Research settlement instruction cut-off times'. As it stands, this is pretty vague and you would have to take the person's word for it that it had been completed. If, however, you add that it will deliver a matrix of the standard and best-effort cut-off times by market by product for all markets and products, it will be eminently clear when the task is complete. By being very precise about the format and content of the deliverable, you also reduce the possibility of someone misinterpreting the task completely. We said it is most acute in the user community because users are typically not used to working to such formal documentation standards as the IT camp and think that because a fact is obvious to them, it will be readily apparent to everyone. Most project planning tools will have a facility to specify deliverables by task.

Milestones

Milestones should be inserted in the project plan to signify the completion of a major component or phase of a project. Just like real milestones, they should be highly visible and readily understood by a broad audience. Again, like real milestones, they should provide you with a very clear and accurate measure of how far through your journey you are and how much further you have to go. Used in a project plan, they are a way of ignoring the clutter of the underlying tasks and simply demonstrating progress towards the end goal. They are particularly useful for reporting to senior management who only need to concern themselves with the end objective and not the route by which it is reached. To use the example of the medieval traveller on his way to the City of London to make his fortune in the world of merchant banking, it doesn't matter how many highwaymen he has to fend off or how many rivers he has to ford along the way, if he isn't at a specified milestone when he planned to be, he is unlikely to reach his destination on time. And the nearer he gets to his destination, the less likely still he will be able to make up time. Project milestones should reflect exactly the same thing and late arrival at any milestone should start alarm bells ringing.

Milestones should be used at regular intervals throughout the project schedule and particularly in the early stages. The early tasks of a project are normally those most likely to be delayed while resources are still being brought on board, tasks are still being assigned etc. and how often is it said 'We'll make it up later'. Well-placed milestones in the preliminary stages will confirm whether any early slippage has been made up and if not, will get it escalated for senior management's attention. As a rule of thumb, you might be able to make up time between milestones but not across them, i.e. late arrival at one milestone will delay arrival at the next by at least a similar amount unless you have built in contingency which we will discuss next.

Contingency

In order to cushion against the unforeseen, it is normal practice to incorporate some contingency within project schedules. Contingency is basically time and effort which you haven't planned to use but is incorporated into the schedule as though it will be used.

There are many ways of incorporating contingency but the simplest way is to add some between your scheduled completion time and the corresponding milestone so that if all goes well, you will reach your milestone ahead of schedule. And because the milestone represents a significant stage of the journey, you can be sure you really are ahead. Almost just as importantly, it is a way of managing expectations of project sponsors. They will feel much happier with milestones being reached ahead of schedule than continually over-running.

Contingency should always be used with care otherwise it can quickly become absorbed into the scheduled available time. If individual tasks overrun, the overrun must be addressed and its significance impressed upon the people concerned. Contingency is like an insurance policy and is there to mitigate against the unexpected (Figure 4.13). You don't leave your house with doors and windows unlocked knowing you can claim for any theft on your household insurance, and similarly you don't accept consistent overrunning of completion dates on the basis that you can take it out of your contingency fund!

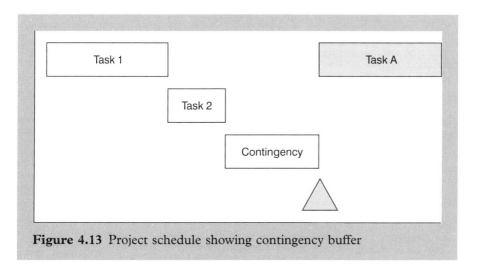

Figure 4.13 Project schedule showing contingency buffer

One final note on contingency: don't confuse it with resource availability. If you assign a resource to a task full time, taking account of holidays, training and sickness, as a rough rule of thumb, they will only be productive for four days out of five, i.e. a task estimated to require four days of effort will, on average, take five days to complete. This extra day is not a day's contingency, it is just taking account of predictable staff availability by averaging out total absences over the year. However, you also have to be wary of this approach as it means when the resource is on a task without any intervening absences, they should finish, for example, a four-day task in four days rather than the scheduled five. This progress ahead of schedule will, of course, be absorbed next time they are absent but over the long term it should mean they are exactly on target.

An alternative approach is to specifically schedule in holidays and training but you cannot schedule sickness and the additional administrative tasks create a lot of noise on the schedule.

Project tracking

Project tracking is about knowing where you are in reality relative to where your schedule says you should be theoretically. It is the most important part of project management because unless you know you are going adrift from your original plan, you won't be able to take corrective action to get back on-course. This was always a problem for the ancient seafarers, knowing where they were at a point in time relative to their map and it is the same for the modern project manager – knowing where he or she is relative to their schedule. Most importantly, it is about knowing how much longer it is going to take you to reach your final destination and at what cost.

There are two key aspects to assessing your current position relative to your original schedule – distance travelled and cost incurred – and we look at these more closely in the following sections. As these two aspects are measured historically, they are absolute and can therefore pinpoint your position on the schedule with a fair degree of accuracy. But although they will tell you how far you have come, and by deduction, how far there is to go, they won't tell you how long it will take or how much more it will cost. This is where you have to feed the results of your journey so far into your revised forecasts for the remainder of the journey assuming you will progress against the plan at the same relative rate as you have done historically. That is, if you have only made three-quarters of the speed you anticipated so far, it is prudent to assume you will only make three-quarters speed for the remainder of the journey.

When you set out on your project journey, like a map, you have to start on the premise that it is a true and accurate description of where you are going and how long it is going to take you. Prior to starting out, you must lock the schedule in place so that you have a fixed datum against which to measure progress. This is known as 'baselining' the schedule and is supported by most, if not all, project management software. Remember, a project schedule is a working document and will need to be reviewed and adjusted in the light of actual progress. However, you must be aware of how the revisions relate to the original schedule so that you can see whether you are remaining on the same path or drifting away from it. If you were to continually review a schedule without being able to relate it to the original, you would quickly lose track of your overall direction and would have no idea whether you were still on schedule.

Progress against plan

The first aspect of project tracking we will look at is actual progress against planned progress. That is, if our plan says we should have completed tasks A, B and C by the end of the month, at the end of the month we take stock of what has actually been completed and compare it to what we forecast would be completed.

If our actual progress matches the plan, it means our plan was accurate and we could therefore assume that the rest of the plan will also be completed to schedule. However, in reality we may come across unforeseen problems in the latter half of the project that slow progress but we cannot predict this. Therefore we tend to make the assumption that if our estimates proved accurate in the first half of the project, that same level of accuracy will prevail throughout. If our actual progress is ahead of our planned progress, then it might be tempting to assume we will get ahead of ourselves in the latter half but again this may be far from the reality of the situation. There is no telling that we are going to be as fortunate going forward as we have been looking back and it is therefore prudent to stick to the original schedule and hopefully finish ahead of time.

If we are unfortunate and find ourselves behind schedule, while it is not what we would want, the important point is that we have recognized we are adrift from the plan and can therefore set about taking corrective measures. Assessing progress is a very emotional subject and typically, especially in the high-pressure environment of a project meeting, no one likes to admit or accept they are behind schedule. This reluctance to admit to being behind schedule can be very damaging for the project as slippage is hidden and therefore no corrective action can be taken. In our experience, people are always going to finish tasks 'the following day' – this takes the heat off them in the meeting and as a result makes it look as if everything is in order. This brings us back to the earlier section where we looked at tasks and deliverables. By ensuring all tasks have a clearly defined deliverable, you can take the emotion out of progress reporting and assess completion unequivocally by the presence or absence of the specified deliverable. This is why deliverable definitions are so important for measuring progress because they take the judgement factor out of what constitutes a completed task – if it ain't there, it ain't complete. Another trap we have seen project managers fall foul of is the line 'it is complete except for . . .'. It pays to take a hard line in these situations and if there is an 'except for . . .', then it ain't complete and is behind schedule.

We all get tempted to take an optimistic view of projects and how they are progressing. The number of times we have seen project managers marking a task as complete because Mr X is confident it will be completed by next week and he is a reliable sort of chap etc, etc. Be warned: there is no place for optimism (or pessimism) in project tracking. Optimism is for planning and forecasting tracking is absolute and progress must be reported accordingly.

Cost against budget

The second aspect of project tracking that we're going to look at is cost. Because cost is absolute and reported independently through the management accounts, it cannot be influenced (at least not unwittingly) by peoples' sense of pride or emotions. Having said that, it is important to make sure appropriate accounting systems are in place from the outset to ensure time and materials are correctly attributed. Also there is no judgement factor involved when it comes to cost accounting, unlike progress reporting. For example, a project manager may claim to be half-way through a project and on target to complete on time, all the tasks to the half-way stage supposedly being complete. However, when you look at the cost versus budget, this shows three-quarters of the budget has already been spent, suggesting another three-quarters is still required, implying a cost overrun of 50%! So although things are on schedule, they are only on schedule because additional resources have been sucked in to keep up. Cost overruns are the most apparent symptoms of a project running into difficulties and should be monitored very closely to give an early warning that things are not as they should be. If your cost versus budget is in line with your progress against plan then you can be confident that you are where you think you are.

Typical problems

We mention here some of the typical problems we have seen or experienced on projects of various sizes over the years.

Unavailability of key users

During the initial stages of user requirements definition, IT business analysts require access to a large number of keys users who are notoriously difficult to get hold of and so the production of finalized user requirements definitions are invariably delayed. This has a knock-on effect to the downstream tasks which are all dependent on receiving finalized user requirement definitions upon which to base their developments. However, because of the amount of IT resources which would be left idle if they were to wait for completed requirements, they often continue on the basis of incomplete requirements definitions and the project is still reported to be on schedule. Focus then shifts to the succeeding tasks and the gaps in requirements are never completed because the business analysts have already moved on to new tasks. We now have a situation where the project appears to be on schedule but in fact has missing requirements which will rear their ugly heads further down the road when they will be that much more expensive to incorporate.

As we discussed earlier, progress is absolute and if a task is not 100% complete then it is not finished and any successor tasks should be held until it is. Otherwise, there is no point in putting complex dependencies in the schedule if we are just going to ignore them to avoid reporting lack of progress. In practice, this is a difficult thing to do as no one wants to leave expensive resources sitting idle. However, at the same time it is dangerous to delude ourselves that we can continue with subsequent stages of the project without fully completing preceding tasks. It is much better to sound a warning at the outset than wait for it to bite you when you're least expecting it and when it is most disruptive. Remember: user requirements can be changed at the stroke of a pen but their impact on systems design may take months of reworking.

95% complete

Typically you will find that on any piece of work, progress to 95% completion will be reached very early on but the last 5% will drag on, sometimes past completion date. It is human nature to want to do well and, as we said earlier, out of a combination of pride and embarrassment, people will give an optimistic picture of their progress and it won't be until the deliverable is due that they will be forced to be more realistic. On top of the emotional issue you normally find the last 20% of a task is genuinely more difficult because it involves bringing the whole thing together which in turn means picking up all the problematical issues deferred earlier on. To help avoid overstatement of progress you need to ensure a culture of openness where people are prepared to be honest about their progress even when it is not as good as one would like. We have seen some projects where team members have lived in fear of not meeting their target dates and early on, results appear to be impressive. However, later, when the impact is far worse, you discover things weren't completed as thoroughly as they should have been but were reported as being in order. For the project manager, it is essential to know exactly where you are on the schedule even if it is not to your liking because then, you have the chance to take corrective measures. Shutting your eyes and pretending everything is rosy is just storing up worse problems for later when they will be much harder to deal with and much time and money may have been wasted getting there. As we said earlier, progress is absolute and the project culture should encourage it to be reported as such.

Scope creep

Users have a nasty habit of coming up with additional requirements as the project progresses which naturally will have an adverse impact on progress. It is understandable that this will happen because as users discover the more detailed workings of the system, they will dream up new ideas, many of which will be perfectly sensible. This is where you need to take a very firm line and if it is not needed to achieve the business objective then it should be clearly and publicly ruled out of scope. We say publicly because it is important that everybody is made aware of the situation at the same time to avoid further disputes later on.

We must also be careful to distinguish between scope creep, where we are trying to add new functionality, and unforeseen complexity where it turns out to be more difficult than expected. We accused users earlier of trying to incorporate additional functionality but IT will also try to define unforeseen complexity as additional functionality to justify additional time and cost. Unforeseen complexity is one of the hazards of project management and is very much in scope.

Staff turnover

Particularly on a large project you will be susceptible to staff turnover during the lifetime of the project and the further along the road you are when it happens, the greater the impact. Although it is very difficult you must try to avoid creating 'key' individuals who would leave a void in the knowledge base if they were to walk out. To do this you need to ensure a free flow of information between all project team members and avoid independent secretive silos developing in key areas. The wider you spread the knowledge, the less dependent you are on a single individual and are therefore at less risk of staff turnover.

You should be particularly conscious of projects which are common throughout the industry and where staff are highly mobile. The implementation of the Euro and Y2K are two prime examples of common problems with the same fixed deadline which generated huge amounts of staff turnover as firms struggled to increase their project teams in the run-up to what was an immovable deadline. Thankfully such common challenges do not occur that frequently but there are many subsets of common initiatives such as application software, CSD/ICSD system changes, regulations, etc., which create an industrywide demand for both Operations and IT staff.

Other distractions

Because many projects run over a considerable period of time, there is plenty of opportunity for them to be disrupted by external events. Typically problems on the line desks will distract management attention from projects and even cause resources to be temporarily or permanently withdrawn. Sometimes problems in the line can be caused by the secondment of experienced resources to projects in the first place. When embarking on significant projects you should consider the strength, stability and workload of the line desks. If you are already struggling to keep up with the day-to-day work, you are not in a position to take on additional project work. This will just cause your resources to be spread even more thinly and is likely to result in failure on the line and the project. Unless you are in good shape to start with, you are significantly reducing your chances of success because you have no spare capacity to absorb all the other unforeseen events that will conspire to disrupt the project and the day-to-day activity.

Managing IT suppliers

IT is undoubtedly the biggest and most expensive supplier to the Operations department and its cost will account for a large portion of Operations operating costs passed on to the business. And yet it is generally managed with much less focus than other Operations suppliers such as agent banks, data vendors, communications providers, etc. There has been a tendency on the part of Operations departments (and, we are sure, others) to leave the supply of IT services entirely in the hands of the IT management and yet it is the most critical and expensive service Operations purchase. Whether it is being provided internally or externally, it must be managed with the same discipline and focus as any other service to ensure service quality expectations are met and costs are competitive. Take as an example the agent bank network. Most sizeable Operations departments will have a dedicated network management function whose sole purpose is to monitor and measure service delivery by the banks. They monitor service quality, push for added-value services, claim for losses and, on top of all this, squeeze costs at the same time. If we could apply just some of this discipline to the management of IT suppliers, it can only have a positive effect on overall service delivery. There is a lot of truth in the old saying 'what gets measured gets done'.

We are not suggesting you start hiring dedicated IT service delivery managers, although many large organizations do have programme management teams whose job it is to ensure value for money and timely delivery of IT solutions to the end recipients. What we will discuss in a little more detail is the minimum any user of IT services should be doing to help ensure they get good value for money.

You need to monitor the reliability of the systems quantitatively on an ongoing basis so that you can spot adverse trends before they become a problem. It is also important that the measures are made by the Operations area as IT may not perceive a failure in the same light. For example, a slowdown in system response times may cause operational deadlines to be missed but IT would not necessarily count this, as it did not result in an outright technical failure. The sort of things you need to keep a close eye on are:

- Frequency and length of system downtime on a daily basis, including late opening of the online system
- Number of software bugs outstanding at any one time broken down into new bugs coming to light and old ones being fixed – hopefully they are being fixed quicker than they are being discovered!
- Number of system enhancement requests outstanding – are they growing?
- Cost of external claims directly attributable to software failures
- Transaction volumes and exceptions – in an STP environment you want to make sure exceptions don't become the norm
- Transaction latency – i.e. the average and maximum times transactions are taking to flow through the system

Once you have a monitoring system in place, you can start to identify trends and causal effects of other service failings. For example, perhaps you had many complaints of late confirmations on a particular day that happened to coincide with extraordinary high volumes pointing to a capacity problem. Using these statistics you can have regular review meetings with the IT heads to give them useful feedback on service quality. You can also begin to set performance targets possibly leading to a service level agreement (SLA) which will formalize the supplier/client relationship. We will talk about costs more in the IT Budgets section but will mention them here for completeness. A key indicator of IT system quality is the cost of keeping the system up and running. It is possible you could be getting adequate system reliability but at a cost of armies of support personnel to sustain it. It is therefore imperative that system performance is monitored in conjunction with support costs because cost effectiveness is equally important. Ideally you would want to compare costs with other providers or competitors but apart from being a closely guarded secret, it is difficult to compare like with like because of the many ways different firms account for their IT costs. As a minimum you need to be aware of the cost trends within your own organization.

Supplier relationship

Large organizations will invariably have their own internal IT departments for the provision of corporate IT services but many smaller firms are increasingly looking at outsourcing. In this section we will consider both models and contrast the pros and cons of each.

Internal IT group

There is little doubt that an internal IT provider will have better corporate knowledge and cultural awareness than a supplier operating at arm's length. They will also have a better overall business understanding as the individuals will have probably worked on many different functions within Operations whereas the individual staff members of a supplier will have a much narrower business experience. For example, a supplier of reconciliation packages will have limited experience of the settlement instruction process upon which automated reconciliation very much depends. With internal IT staff, not only is it likely they will have worked on settlement instructions but they will be much better placed to understand the system connectivity between the two functions.

Because internal IT groups charge on a time and materials basis rather than fixed price, they can naturally be more flexible when changing requirements and priorities. In addition, you get dedicated attention as they do not have the distraction of other clients, unlike external providers, who often find themselves trying to cope with conflicting priorities from equally demanding clients.

We also think it is easier to develop a closer and longer-term relationship with internal providers because both parties will share directly in the success of their mutual employer. Although external providers will benefit from your organization's success, the link is not so direct and they can also benefit from the success of their other clients, so it may depend how big a fish you are in their sea!

External IT group

Some organizations have completely outsourced their entire IT operation from desktop support to data centre but nearly all use external providers for at least one or more specific applications. IT services which do not require an intimate understanding of the business are the easiest to outsource and are likely to stand more chance of success. Many firms these days outsource the support of their hardware and network infrastructures to firms specializing in the provision of these services. You don't need to understand the financial operations business to provide a high-availability hardware infrastructure. In fact the provision of such services is a specialist field in its own right and by using an external supplier you will benefit from the experience and economy of scale of them providing it to a broad client base. A good example of this is disaster recovery (DR) where the supplier can share the cost of providing a DR facility across his entire client base. DR provision is a common driver for outsourcing the data centre part of the IT service.

Unfortunately, as you move into the IT services that are more closely intertwined with the business and the personnel of the business, such as application development and business analysis, the case for using external providers becomes less clear-cut. It is relatively easy to specify that you want a hardware platform available 20 hours per day, 365 days per year with a peak capacity of 10 000 transactions per hour. This is fairly definitive whereas asking for an 'equity settlement system' is an order of magnitude more vague and consequently it is much more difficult to define service expectations and costs. Again, it is the services common to all businesses that can be outsourced most effectively such as desktop support where you require expertise in generic PC software rather than business-specific applications.

Because of the difficulties highlighted above, when supplying application software you will have far less flexibility to change things when dealing with external suppliers because they will have their profit margin and reputation to protect. Although it is not in itself a bad thing, you will find user specifications will have to be much more detailed and will have to be basically set in stone before development commences. Any changes in function or priorities will invariably result in additional cost and delayed completion dates because the supplier also has other clients to service and cannot afford to disrupt their schedules as a result of your changes. You may even find you can't get enhancements done at all due to commitments the supplier has with other clients, normally new ones who have just been brought on-board and are consequently prioritized for attention by the supplier's management.

On the plus side, you may get fixed price terms for smaller changes and you don't need to maintain a large IT resource pool on standby for enhancement work. Against that you will not get the level of corporate knowledge and the continuity of IT resources you will have from an in-house department.

With a stable, easy-to-define service such as the supply of hardware infrastructure there are clearly benefits in outsourcing to a specialist supplier who can provide higher levels of efficiency through economy of scale. Similarly, the more static nature of retail banking, point of sale, supply chain control systems, etc. make them more appropriate for outsourcing to specialist third-party providers whose core competence is running and supporting high-availability systems. Conversely, the highly dynamic nature of the financial operations business where requirements and priorities can change intra-day requires a much more flexible and responsive IT service to support it. In addition, this environment requires flexibility and responsiveness in a joint Operations and IT service delivery that would be difficult to achieve if the two groups work for different organizations and have different objectives. In-house IT functions working alongside the Operations group are more likely to pull out all the stops and, dare we say it, take risks in order to exploit fleeting business opportunities than an external provider would. An internal IT group has the same business objectives as those of the fund manager or investment bank they work for and that is to do whatever is necessary to support the business in making money which, from time to time, will require service above the call of duty and calculated risk taking. An external

IT provider's objectives are to make money for their own organization and the way he does this is by providing a robust, reliable and consistent service. He is not inclined to take chances because he is not rewarded for risks and in fact is likely to be penalized if things go wrong. By taking chances he loses both ways because he doesn't benefit particularly from successful exploitation of the client's business opportunity and he is penalized if things go wrong as a result – in banking terms there is no risk–reward premium in it so why should he do it?

IT support structure

Assuming an in-house IT function there are basically two structures with which IT can support the Operations desks: shared pool or dedicated specialist teams. Whichever structure is employed, there will always be certain functions that have to be provided on a centralized basis. We already spoke about hardware and network infrastructures being common across the corporation but we can also include database administration and e-commerce. These functions need to be centralized to ensure interoperability between functional applications and consistency of standards and, in the case of e-commerce, corporate image. You wouldn't want each business function having its own database with all the data duplication that would lead to just as you wouldn't want them to have their own style of website.

Because of the many and varied specialist technical skills required to develop modern Operations systems, a shared pool structure is the most efficient way of delivering IT services. You will find that each functional application requires an amount of particular technical skills that can be utilized in any functional area and can thus be sourced from a common pool. As they finish one application, they will automatically be assigned to the next one which will require the same technical knowhow but may be in a completely different functional area. The main criticism of this approach is that the IT people don't get a chance to build any in-depth business knowledge and need to work from more detailed specifications which reduces responsiveness. Dedicated IT teams aligned with business functions are favoured by users because the increased business specialization they gain makes the communication of user requirements much more efficient and less error-prone. At the same time, the IT and user teams develop a closer, more cooperative relationship working to common goals. Provided the user function is large enough and generates enough work to justify a self-contained IT support group, this is without doubt the most efficient operating structure. When operating in this dedicated support group mode, you need to make sure the appropriate control mechanisms are in place to keep the independent groups working to the same business and technical strategy. Because the users and IT develop such close relationships they can, with the best of intentions, easily deviate from their corporate strategy in pursuit of their own localized objectives. However, while users always prefer this unified team approach, IT technicians may not. They won't necessarily want to specialize in a particular business function and would be more concerned about working with the latest technology.

Operations drive IT

The most important thing to establish in any Operations–IT relationship is that the business drives Operations which drives IT – in the cut and thrust environment of capital markets there is no other way for it to work. To put it bluntly, and we are talking here about in-house providers, IT are not employed to learn and play with the latest technology fad to stimulate their own interest and enhance their own personal technical profile. As we have emphasized throughout this book, any and every IT change or fix must be supported by a sound business rationale. Even things considered to be purely technical, such as operating system upgrades, must have a robust business case and must be sanctioned and prioritized by the user.

In a large enough organization, there is a role for genuine research into new technology but it must be recognized for what it is and be subject to the normal project disciplines such as objectives, target dates and budgets. Even then it should have some sort of business case to justify the expenditure but the case is likely to be far from conclusive as the results must, by the nature of research, be unpredictable.

IT for their part need to develop an IT strategy that will not only support the corporate business strategy but will also be compliant with the many external industry initiatives with which Operations have to work. For example, external communication has traditionally been by store and forward of discrete messages, file transfer or a combination of both representing the lowest common technological denominator. However, with the increasing use of Internet Protocol (IP) for communication in a true real-time environment, systems have to be designed from the ground up to work in this mode. That is rather than sending a message and receiving a report back some time later on the message's progress, you can expect to have a response fired back immediately, which your systems architecture needs to be able to handle. If this type of capability is not designed in from day one, it is almost impossible to upgrade to this level of real-time processing later. Gone are the days when your systems could be insulated from the outside world by file transfers and store and forward communication protocols. They now have to interact seamlessly in real-time with the myriad external client and supplier systems around the world and they have to do it even more reliably. It is therefore critical that you have an IT strategy that will keep you compliant with technology trends across the industry if you are to maintain compatibility.

Setting priorities

As soon as you have excess demand over supply you have to make decisions and prioritize the demands in order of benefit. In our experience demands on IT have always exceeded supply and therefore concise prioritization of demands is key to the effective use of IT. Like any service provider, IT can only do so much in any given timeframe and must be given clear guidance on what needs doing first and when it needs to be done by. Unless Operations provide this guidance, IT will prioritize according to their view of the world, which will be based more on system logic than or hard business requirements.

There was a time when we used to treat bugs and enhancements separately for the purpose of prioritization on the basis that bugs are faults to the status quo and therefore need to be fixed immediately whereas enhancements are changing the status quo and should be subject to prioritization. This proved unsuccessful for a few reasons. First, most systems have too many outstanding bugs to be fixed immediately and so, sadly, they have to be prioritized within the definition of 'immediate'. Second, bugs are not necessarily that critical and once known about can often be circumvented through user procedures. Lastly, whether it is categorized as a bug or an enhancement, the IT work will generally need to be carried out by the same resources who can only work on one thing at a time. More recently we have started to treat bugs and enhancements in the same way as far as prioritization is concerned. If someone discovers a bug in an application, they need to justify the fixing of it just as if they were asking for an enhancement. Just because a piece of software fails to work as it should and is therefore classified as a bug, if it is not disadvantaging the underlying business then there is no business case to justify the cost of fixing it. You would be better off using available IT resources to carry out an enhancement that does have a sound business case.

As an example, let us assume our new STP system fails to automatically enrich settlement details in very specific circumstances resulting in a handful of trades going on the repair queue instead of straight through. Although it is clearly a bug, the consequences of it can be controlled through the normal exception processing function so it is not giving rise to any significant increase in risk and the only cost is the manual repair of half a dozen trades each day. If the cost of fixing it is several man-months' work then while it is a bug, it does not warrant automatically being put to the top of the priority list. You would be better off using that several man-months' work to put in an enhancement that's going to give you real savings. By putting bugs and enhancements through the same justification and prioritization process you will ensure that you get best value for money out of your IT spend.

Although we suggest you don't distinguish between bugs and enhancements for the purposes of prioritization, it is important that they are classified as such for monitoring IT service quality and budgeting, which we will consider in the next section.

IT budgets

As one of the biggest Operations' costs, it is essential that the IT spend is budgeted accurately and monitored closely to ensure adherence to budget. Variances in this area will have a disproportionate effect on the overall Operations budget due to its large size relative to the rest of Operations' costs. What we are going to cover here is budgets in relation to IT services specific to the Operations department. General IT infrastructure costs such as network, database administration, desktop support, etc. will normally be allocated according to the corporate management accounting policy and you will have little control over the amount suffered. What you do need to control is your direct IT costs which ideally should be broken down into three categories:

- Standstill
- Enhancements
- Capital projects

Standstill and enhancement costs will be expensed out of the current period's budget as they are costs incurred in the running of the day-to-day business. Although the costs are expensed out of the period in which they are incurred, savings, where relevant, may still be accrued over a number of years. The cost of capital projects, on the other hand, will be accumulated as work in progress on the balance sheet and depreciated over their useful life starting from the point when they are first implemented.

Standstill

As a starting point you need to know the absolute minimum expenditure you will need to make on IT services purely to keep the systems running in their existing state. Under this heading there is no allowance for any sort of enhanced functionality, it covers only the essential work that needs to be carried out to keep the systems running on a day-to-day basis. The things you will need to budget for in the standstill category are:

- Hardware maintenance – you will need to have maintenance contracts in place to cover hardware failures and these normally vary in cost according to the period you need cover and response times required. For example, 24-hour, 1-hour on-site will be more expensive than 8:00 am to 6:00 pm with a 3-hour on-site response.
- Third-party software maintenance – there will be an annual licensing fee plus a maintenance fee according to the cover you require.
- Third-party software version upgrades – you will often find version upgrades are charged in addition to general maintenance and can be very expensive. In theory they should be optional but you will eventually find the supplier will only support the current and last few versions so you can find yourself forced into an expensive upgrade.
- In-house application support – as you pay for a maintenance contract for third-party suppliers so you will need to pay a support cost for in-house-developed applications. The benefit of the in-house fee is that support resources can be working on enhancements if there is no critical support work to be done.
- System software upgrades – upgrades to system software, budgeted at the corporate level, will at a minimum necessitate

application regression testing and at worst may require an application upgrade.

To summarize, you are trying to arrive at the minimum IT expenditure assuming no enhanced functionality will be required. While this figure is a little unrealistic in practice because you will undoubtedly require some changes over the budget period, it does give you a feel for how efficient your IT systems are. If you are suffering a high standstill cost then it probably means the quality and reliability of the systems are low because you are incurring high support costs.

One thing to look out for with packaged software is how industry or regulatory changes, which you have no choice over, are covered by the maintenance contracts. For example, when SWIFT moved from the ISO 7775 to the ISO 15022 securities message standard, many vendors charged separately for their products to be upgraded to the new formats even though they would have stopped working if it wasn't done!

When negotiating this budget with IT, take a firm stance. They will naturally try to create a small profit in this area to give them more flexibility and buffer themselves from unforeseen problems. Use historical trends on system reliability to assess proposed support levels. If the previous year has passed with a low incidence of system failure then, assuming no major changes, you would expect support costs to be on the low side. If, on the other hand, the incidence of failure has been high, then your support cost budget will have to reflect this until you can get the reliability up to standard, which will be an issue in its own right.

Enhancements

By enhancement we mean a change to the system that will make it do something over and above what it currently does. Notice we said 'what it does' and not what it was supposed to do. Once a system is in production it is not worth concerning ourselves with what it should have done, all we have to go on is what it does now as far as enhancements are concerned. That is, even though the functionality may have been in the original specification, if it was left out at implementation then, if it is still warranted, it becomes an enhancement. Although a system will keep functioning in its current state without enhancements it may stop fulfilling the business requirements, hence you cannot assume all enhancements are optional. Some enhancements are more essential to the wellbeing of the business than bug fixes to the status quo. We have found it very useful to classify enhancements into two broad categories of discretionary and non-discretionary to help to facilitate the prioritization process.

Non-discretionary enhancements

Non-discretionary in this instance means there is an overwhelming business case in favour of it, not that it is part of standstill. Within non-discretionary we find it helpful again to categorize by principal driver:

- Regulatory/industry – if you need to change your systems to comply with regulatory or industry changes then unless you exit the affected businesses, you are going to have to comply and get the enhancement done.
- New business – if the change is necessary to support a new business initiative that has already been sanctioned then it is very likely the enhancement will have to be made with the cost coming from the new business start-up budget

In broad terms you can basically forget discretionary changes until all the non-discretionary enhancements have been taken care of and within non-discretionary, you'd better look at the regulatory and industry-driven ones ahead of the others.

Discretionary enhancements

Discretionary enhancements are truly optional and will be prioritized on the basis of the value they add to the business, which basically takes the form of increased efficiency or risk mitigation. If necessary, all enhancements in this category can be put on the back burner and the associated budget saved. However, if there is a compelling commercial case for them and the payback is within the budget period, expenditure here could be more than offset by the savings accrued, potentially resulting in a lower budget overall. The reason for distinguishing between enhancements for efficiency and enhancements for risk mitigation is that they need to be assessed on different criteria and by different groups. Efficiency initiatives will generally be approved or rejected in conjunction with the associated business line whereas risk mitigation initiatives will be approved at the corporate level, usually corporate risk management.

- Efficiency – improvements in the level of automation or rationalization of processes that will lead to an outright reduction of costs
- Risk reduction – usually in the form of additional system controls and/or validation that will prevent or at least significantly reduce the likelihood of financial or reputational loss

You will generally find most enhancements fall into the efficiency category as managers strive to improve their levels of STP and reduce costs. Many risk-mitigating initiatives will arise directly as a result of an Operational loss or a very near-miss and will be judged primarily on that basis while it is fresh in peoples' minds. It is an unfortunate fact of life that justification based on the mitigation of an accident waiting to happen is nowhere near as convincing as an accident that has happened.

Capital projects

Large-scale projects, which have a long development time and where the cost is out of proportion to the revenue, are capitalized on the balance sheet until they are implemented. This means the costs incurred in the development do not affect the business until it is implemented, at which point the cost will be amortized over the expected useful life which in the case of software is normally no more than 5 years. The budgets for these projects will be segregated so that the build costs can be accumulated over the period of development without affecting the operating expense line. Of course, once it is implemented and the business is reaping the benefit of the investment, the total cost will be depreciated over its working life to its residual value at the end of its useful life. For example, a company may buy a new van, which has a useful working life of 5 years, by which time it is so unreliable it needs replacing. In this instance, the van will have a residual value at the end of 5 years so the difference between the purchase cost and the residual value is depreciated over the 5 years. That is, the cost of the van is offset against income it earns for the business rather than being taken as a single one-off cost up-front where it would cause large distortions in the profit and loss accounts. Unfortunately, in the case of software, it doesn't have any residual value so the full cost of development has to be borne over its working life. Actual criteria for deciding which projects are capitalized and which are expensed will be determined by the organization's financial accounting policy in conjunction with the Generally Agreed Accounting Principles (GAAP).

Capital projects need to be monitored against budget very closely because the actual costs being incurred may not affect the running costs of the business for several years, by which time it is too late to do anything about them. Because the costs are effectively hidden from the business during the build phase, it is essential that thorough and rigorous monitoring of cost against budget is undertaken to avoid any nasty surprises at the end.

Capital projects are normally associated with major systems overhauls or industry changes such as the implementation of the Euro and the Y2K bug. Because of this there is generally little scope for prioritization as they will be of such a size as to determine their urgency in their own right.

Chapter 5

The project life cycle

Introduction

In the previous chapters we looked at how we go about identifying and justifying technology investments. In this chapter we will examine the various stages of the project life-cycle in which these conceptual ideas are turned into reality. Even the best thought-through technology initiatives will fail to deliver their benefits unless we apply a structured and disciplined approach to their development.

This chapter looks at the project life-cycle from the Operations perspective providing an overview of each stage of the process but with the emphasis on what is required from the user community. It will provide an insight into what is going on within the IT area and highlight those things the Operations' users should be doing and considering.

It is based on a generic project life-cycle model that will vary from one organization to another and project attributes such as size and risk. It is broken down into the following stages, which are examined in turn in the rest of the chapter:

- Scope
- Requirements definition
- Design and build

- Unit testing
- System testing
- Integration testing
- User acceptance testing
- Performance testing
- Regression testing
- Conversion
- Implementation

A lot of time is dedicated to user acceptance testing (UAT) as one would expect and the chapter concludes by looking at two other closely related areas: training, and procedures and controls.

Scope

We talked quite a lot about project scope definitions in Chapter 4 but for completeness we will reiterate a few key points here. The project scope is a high-level definition of the size and content of the proposed system in sufficient detail to enable IT to provide a realistic estimate of development time and cost. It is then for Operations to make sure that the proposed scope includes the necessary functionality to form a cohesive technology solution that will enable them to deliver the underlying business benefit to the business. Unless it is a particularly large project, it is the scope and associated cost–benefit analysis that will be used to seek authorization to proceed to full system build stage.

Requirements definition

This is probably the most important phase of the project life cycle as it is the requirements specification which defines the user–IT understanding of what is required. IT will take the original business requirements definition produced by Operations and expand it into a concise logical definition of what they understand to be required in order to fulfil the business requirement. It is extremely important that Operations read and understand the requirements specification down to the last detail because all subsequent project stages will use this document as the blueprint for what needs to be constructed. Because they are written in a structured logical style, they can be difficult for users to comprehend especially if it is their first exposure to IT projects. Because of this, users can be guilty of not gaining a thorough understanding of what is written down, preferring instead to rely on their perception of IT's understanding gleaned in meetings. We cannot overemphasize the importance of going through requirements specifications with a fine-toothed comb and making sure all I's are dotted and T's are crossed. What may seem like an insignificant error to Operations may become deeply embedded in the system design causing all sorts of problems and delays later on. If you find something is not exactly as you understand it or you consider it to be imprecise, get it cleared up immediately however pedantic it may seem at the time.

For example, a specification may say 'Multiple standing settlement instructions may be held for each client account . . .'. Unless it is explicit, a technical programmer, who knows little about the Operations business, may consider five to be more than ample and unintentionally build in an unacceptable constraint on the number of instructions that can be held. Furthermore, assuming the input screen shows only one instruction at a time, a misunderstanding of this nature is unlikely to come to light until a user tries to set up data for testing system extremities, by which time it is too late.

When reviewing requirements specifications, consider it in the wider context of the whole Operations process to ensure all the peripheral activities that occur from time to time can also be supported. The following are some pointers on what to look out for when reviewing requirements' specifications:

- State explicit numbers for multiple instances of data items and transaction volumes

- Make sure those little nuances that only happen very rarely are included and clearly specified
- Make sure that exceptions falling out of the main process flow can be handled manually within the confines of the system and its controls
- Ensure query functionality will support the *ad hoc* vague queries you typically receive from irate traders and counterparts

It is very useful to conduct a walk-through of the requirement's specification again to make sure there is no misunderstanding between IT and Operations. People will often explain things verbally differently from how they would in writing and so it provides another opportunity to uncover misinterpretations or clear up any ambiguities.

Design and build

This is the phase of the project where concepts are turned into reality through the development of input/enquiry screens, transactions and databases. The design phase will map the requirements defined in the requirements specification into the technical components of the system comprising:

- Input/enquiry screens including validation rules, functionality, content layout and interaction behaviour
- Database tables, data relationships, data items, data codes and data integrity rules
- Transaction definitions including data transcription, data enrichment, calculations and input/output interfaces
- Exception condition capture, routing and handling

Much of the technical design is of little consequence to the user as long as it supports the business requirements specified in the previous phase. However, the points at which the system interfaces with human operators, namely screens and reports, are of critical significance and should be the focus for close attention. An IT technician can design the most beautifully aesthetic screen that carries out the required functionality to the letter but is totally impractical as far as usability is concerned. For example, the fields may in the wrong order for logical and rapid data entry, enquiries may force you to scroll or drill down every time to see the data pertinent to the user's needs, search fields may be badly chosen, etc.

You want to get an early view of user interfaces and preferably work with IT in their initial design, to ensure you end up with a workable, efficient operator interface. Although problems would be picked up in user acceptance testing, first, it will most probably cause delays as users wrestle with an impractical interface as well as an unfamiliar system and, second, it will necessitate a significant amount of retesting. Furthermore, we have also experienced occasions where what has seemed like a trivial screen layout change to the user has resulted in major reprogramming which has then impacted underlying functional behaviour. Sometimes the screen layout and user interaction logic are deeply embedded in the core functionality making format changes very difficult to implement.

It is also beneficial to maintain an ongoing dialogue between relevant Operations personnel and the programmers because however good the specifications are, there will always be room for misinterpretation and unsolicited artistic licence by the technicians. If a rapport can be built up between the two then many of these potential deviations from the specification can be prevented ahead of UAT proper. A really effective way of achieving this is to sit the technicians and users at the same desk because it is amazing how much knowledge is communicated in both directions simply by overhearing odd comments here and there. Also, people are more likely to go to the trouble to verify their interpretation if they can talk to someone across the desk rather than if they have to pick up the phone or walk across the office.

Testing overview

In this section we are going to look at the various stages of testing systems, many of which Operations will not be directly involved in but will want to be sure they are carried out. Depending on size and complexity, systems are generally tested in the following phases:

- Unit testing
- System testing
- Integration testing
- User acceptance testing

This is a bottom-up approach, starting with the testing of individual system components, linking them together to test systems, linking these to test system interoperability before finally reaching the user acceptance testing stage when the system and all its interactions are tested in their entirety.

Figure 5.1 shows how testing moves from the inside out encompassing and integrating with more and more systems until the user

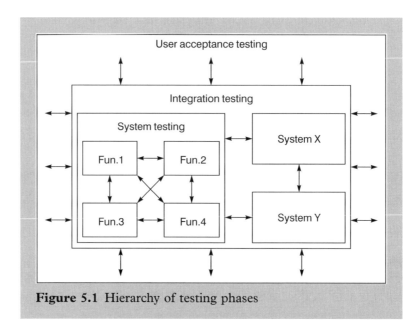

Figure 5.1 Hierarchy of testing phases

acceptance testing stage when the system is really being tested against the business environment itself. We will look briefly at the first three stages of testing but will examine in detail the user acceptance stage where Operations play a crucial role in ensuring the system is both functional and practical before accepting it into day-to-day operation.

In addition to these four basic stages, we will also consider performance testing, or stress testing as it is sometimes known, in which we verify that the system can cope with the workload of live running. Finally, because it will be necessary to make software changes throughout every stage of testing, we describe how we perform regression testing to ensure that functions already tested satisfactorily are not adversely impacted by later changes.

Unit testing

During the technical design phase, the system will be broken down into discrete functional components designed to carry out specific operations on data input to them and provide enriched results as output. Once the programmer has finished coding the required functionality, he will test his code in isolation using the system and design specifications to simulate the expected input and check the desired output (see Figure 5.2).

The programmer is essentially verifying that the function adheres to the specification. Although unit testing is an essential part of the overall test process, because it is done in isolation it is at the mercy of the programmers' interpretation of the requirements and design specification. If the programmer has interpreted something in-correctly, then because the same interpretation will be applied to both the coding and the testing, it will not come to light in unit testing. Unit testing will ensure the coding is robust and integral but does not guarantee adherence to the correct interpretation of

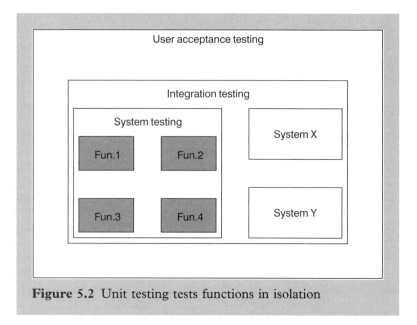

Figure 5.2 Unit testing tests functions in isolation

the business requirement. That is why it is very beneficial if Operations personnel can be involved and at least have an early sight of the unit test plan and results so that any major divergence from the true requirement can be picked up at the earliest possible time.

System testing

Following the successful completion of unit testing, it is then necessary to test that the individual functional components, which will have invariably been programmed by different people, work together as a system. Each functional component, or module as they are often referred to, needs to receive specific data from other modules, carry out some processing on that data and produce enriched data for input to other modules (see Figure 5.3).

Theoretically, system testing is not concerned with verifying the specific functioning of individual modules as this will have already

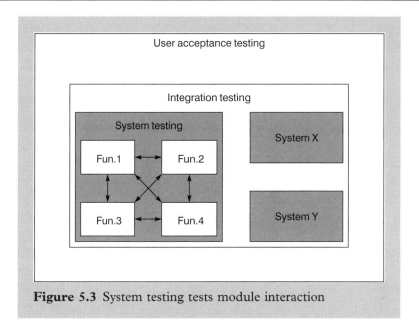

Figure 5.3 System testing tests module interaction

been done in the unit-testing phase. It is concerned more with ensuring that the individual modules receive and produce the correct data in the correct format so that they function as a cohesive whole. This is best illustrated by a simple example.

Let us assume that we have a module that accepts a trade date from a screen, verifies that it is a valid date and passes it to another module to calculate the settlement date. These modules may work perfectly well in the unit-testing phase but fail in the system test because the first one passes the trade date in the format 'ddmmyy' while the programmer who coded the settlement date derivation module assumed that he would receive the date in 'yymmdd' format. So, while each module performs its function perfectly in isolation, the system as a whole is flawed. In reality the problems will be much subtler but it does illustrate the types of error the system-testing process is designed to unearth. It should be noted that system testing only proves the individual components interact in a mechanically compatible way. The data they are communicating may be functionally incorrect but if it is in the right format then the error will not necessarily be highlighted. Using the previous example, it is quite possible that the first module is passing **input date** rather than trade date which the settlement date derivation module would find perfectly acceptable because it is in the correct format but could produce an incorrect settlement date as a result. This is a good example of a subtle error which can be extremely difficult to detect. Because trade and input date are nearly always the same, in most cases settlement date will still be calculated correctly and will only be wrong on those exceptional occasions when a trade is input the next day. You can also see that while the settlement date derivation module is 100% correct with its settlement date derivation, if it is passed the wrong date to start with, technically it will produce the correct settlement date but practically it will be wrong!

Integration testing

Integration testing is basically about ensuring inter-system compatibility and very often will encompass systems that are not involved in the immediate change. Similar to system testing, here we are making sure that the various systems receive and provide data in a compatible and consistently interpreted format (Figure 5.4).

In integration testing we need to verify that the corporations systems as a whole continue to work with the new or amended systems. Even though a system has not been altered itself, it may be adversely impacted by new or changed data emanating from the system that has undergone change. Continuing with the same example, we would want to be sure that our new trade capture system passes the correctly formatted trade date to the General Ledger (GL) for our contingent accounting entries. Even though the chart of accounts may be unchanged, we could find that trade date is being passed in the wrong format or that in fact the GL was receiving settlement date, although this would be harder to detect at this stage.

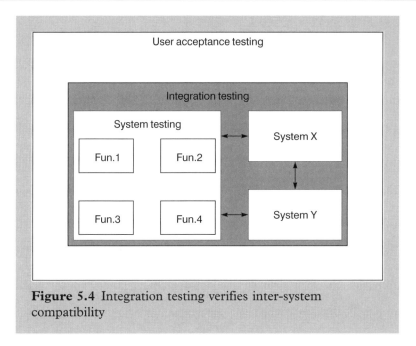

Figure 5.4 Integration testing verifies inter-system compatibility

Integration testing is a higher-level technical test of overall inter-system compatibility and will include the testing of overnight batch schedules and, where possible, testing with external systems which may also be adversely affected by subtle changes in data content and format.

At the completion of integration testing, we need to have a robust, compatible systems environment, which will reliably and consistently process a transaction from initial input through to reconciliation. Only at this point should the system be given over to the users for so-called user acceptance testing (UAT). Systems handed over for UAT may contain functional errors and/or misinterpretations but there is no excuse for handing over a system that does not work mechanically. We have seen systems handed over for UAT which fundamentally do not work, rendering it impossible to test even their functional compliance let alone find any errors. This is extremely frustrating for users and very bad for IT's credibility.

User acceptance testing

User acceptance testing is a structured and controlled simulation of real life, carried out by the users to determine whether the system is acceptable for use in a production environment. It is not just a retest of functions already tested by IT, it is more a test of how the system copes with all the vagaries and nuances of conducting business in the real world which is why it must be carried out by experienced Operations personnel (Figure 5.5).

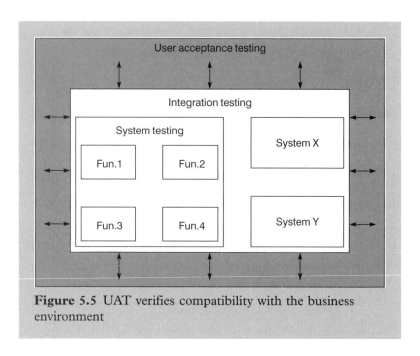

Figure 5.5 UAT verifies compatibility with the business environment

It is impossible to cover 100% of the functionality and it should not be necessary anyway, for reasons previously described. The main focus of the users needs to be on those things that may not be readily apparent to IT and which are difficult to encapsulate in requirements specifications, namely:

■ For any given transaction, verify that **every** aspect of the whole system functions correctly

- Make sure the system is practical to operate in terms of usability and control
- All business nuances can be handled within the confines and integrity of the system even if it is as an exception

This means using a structured approach to creating test conditions, which will simulate a representative sample of business nuances to be conducted in a realistic business and operating situation. At the same time as you are verifying the systems accuracy and integrity, you should be developing and testing operational procedures and controls to be implemented at the same time as the system. However good the system is, you will need to develop desk procedures to ensure Operations personnel know what their new duties are together with the necessary controls to make sure they are carried out.

The rest of this section looks at how you go about preparing for and carrying out the UAT process including the development of new procedures and controls.

The UAT environment

We want to make the UAT as realistic as possible in terms of the simulated environment, data and transactions but at the same time need to structure it to satisfy certain test conditions. This requires an enormous amount of preparation in advance of actual testing to ensure that the test cycle is logically compatible from start to finish. The complex thing about UAT is that business conditions created on the first simulated business day will be used to test further conditions in the second day, third day, etc. and so all reference and transaction data used throughout the cycle must be synchronized to itself and the simulated operating environment. One of the key objectives of UAT is to ensure that the system maintains integrity from one business day to the next and that it can cope with other calendar-based conditions such as bank holidays. To ensure the whole UAT remains together, we need to build our UAT environment in a series of layers, each

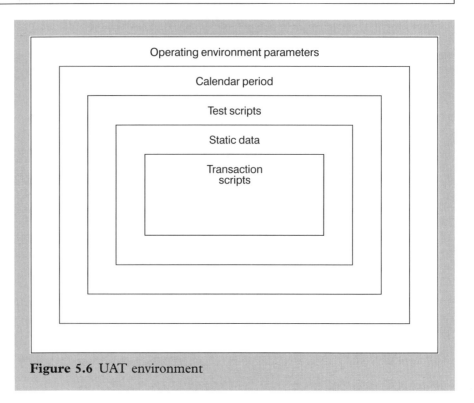

Figure 5.6 UAT environment

layer basing its parameters on those in the previous one. Figure 5.6 shows the various layers we need to consider.

The figure shows how, working from the outside in, we gradually build up a structured test scenario culminating in the definition of individual data values in the centre. It is essential that each layer is defined in this order and fixed for the duration of UAT as each subsequent layer will base its scenario creation on the parameters defined in the outer layers. We will now look at each layer in more detail.

Operating environment parameters

In order to prepare these conditions in advance, we have to define what we call the UAT operating parameters which basically define the simulated working environment in which the UAT will be conducted. In this definition we include business dates, bank holidays, month-ends, year-ends, user access profiles and any other operating environment parameters you wish to simulate. A lot of thought needs to go into this because if you get it wrong, it may preclude the testing of conditions later by which time it will be too late to rectify because the scenario will have already been built up on unsuitable parameters. For example, it may be necessary for you to test your system over an extended bank holiday such as Christmas or you may want to test it over a leap year to verify accrual calculations – these need to be considered up-front and the time period set accordingly. Similarly you may have some sophisticated access control rules you need to test in which case you need to make sure certain transactions are input by a particular profile and amended by another.

Before commencing UAT you also need to define your acceptance criteria. It is highly unlikely you will ever achieve a 100% success rate on any particular test business day so you need to specify thresholds which must be achieved before moving on to the next test business day. Similarly you may specify thresholds below which you will want to rerun the whole test business day from the start. Getting the quality expectations clear will help to prevent acceptance standards being diluted when you start to come under time pressure to cut testing and move on to the next test day.

Calendar period

Once we have set the framework for the overall UAT scenario, we then need to think about how many business days we need to simulate and what the dates of those business days will be. You need to think ahead to the underlying conditions that you need to cover and make sure the number of business days and their dates, relative to each other and the overall calendar, are compatible. For example, you may want to see a trade partially settled across year-end to ensure entries are posted to the correct accounting period, in which case you will need at least two business days before year-end and one after to facilitate the construction of this condition.

Apart from configuring test scenarios around specific calendar dates, you will also have to consider how many business days you need to run. Some complex test conditions may need to be performed across multiple business days so you need to incorporate enough days into your schedule to accommodate these types of tests and we would recommend you allow an extra day just in case of problems.

Because of the limitation of time, it will almost certainly be necessary to jump many days from one test business day to the next in order to achieve date-specific conditions. Some systems do not cater for this and need to be run on consecutive days so you should check this in conjunction with the IT people. In fact, IT and Operations need to work closely to ensure that the UAT calendar not only meets Operations' requirements but can also be supported technically.

Test scripts

Having defined the UAT scenario framework you are now in a position to expand on the detailed test scripts. There are many different opinions on what a test script is and the level of detail it is defined at so this is our personal view of how to construct them. As stated earlier, the purpose of UAT is to simulate real-life working and to incorporate all the imperfections and anomalies that real life entails because these are the aspects which cannot be apparent to IT. Rather than focusing at the detail level, it should focus on the end-to-end processing of the transaction life cycle across a representative calendar period. Most UAT scripts will span several business days as they will often need one or more business days to set up the conditions necessary to carry out the test. For example, if you want to test back-valued settlement postings, you will need one business day to set up the trade, one day for failed settlement and then one day to do the back-valued posting.

This is where it starts to become complex and difficult to track because one script will require various actions on multiple business days and if any action is carried out incorrectly, it will prevent you from executing the intended test. It is essential that you employ a disciplined approach to the construction of test scripts so that they can be linked to underlying test data, tracked throughout their life cycle and assigned to an owner who is responsible for execution and checking. There is not enough space here to go into test scripts in detail but we have set out some guidance notes which should help to keep you on-course:

- Document test scripts in a central file that can be accessed by the whole UAT team – packages are available for this.
- Each script should be self-contained in that it defines a specific test objective and the conditions necessary to perform it.
- Every script should have a unique reference that can be carried through to the test data.
- An owner should be assigned to each script who is responsible for its execution.
- All aspects of a script should be checked in every run even where it is not part of the actual test – this ensures the ultimate test isn't corrupted by earlier failures.
- For scripts requiring many runs to complete, include two or more instances of the same script in case of corruption mid-way through.
- Make sure each owner's scripts are isolated from external influences by using segregated static data (see later).
- Keep the number of scripts to a minimum to avoid the 'wood for the trees' syndrome.
- Each script must have a precisely defined expected result which can leave no ambiguity as to its success – it's either right or wrong.

Once the test scripts are defined logically, they then need to be created in the systems environment by enriching them with the appropriate static and transactional data which takes us into the test data creation stages.

Static data

Some people like to take copies of production data for use in UAT rather than set up specific data from scratch. This is acceptable but you need to extract a structured subset, which you will need to tweak to create the necessary scenarios and fit in with the overall UAT parameters. The subset should be as small as possible and then allocated to specific owners for use in constructing the data for their test scripts. Script owners can then amend their subset of static data to suit their needs without impacting anyone else's test environment. Depending on the systems involved, UAT testers will have their own instruments, counterparts, trading books, currencies and user profiles to ensure as much insulation as possible from other testing. Each owner then has total responsibility for checking all aspects of system functionality within their universe of static data. Where functionality crosses these boundaries, such as a failed trade report, each owner is still responsible for checking their subset of data within the overall function.

What you want to avoid at all cost is a scattergun usage of static data which results in scripts being corrupted by other tester's static data changes or the effect of their transactions, and results not being checked because ownership cannot be clearly established. Keep to a focused, optimal set of static data that satisfies your scenarios but at the same time is limited in size and can be tightly controlled.

Transaction scripts

Using the operating environment parameters, calendar period, test scripts and static data already defined, you can construct the necessary transaction data to implement your test conditions. As mentioned earlier, one script may require the execution of many functions over several business days so you need to establish a way of linking all the components together. This is best illustrated by a simple example:

Test ref: GSB-01
Test name: Failed trade reporting
Test objective: Open trades only to be reported on failed trade report on the business day immediately after value date.

Actual day	Business date (run)	Action	Expected results
2/5/02	16/12/02 (1)	Input new trade for settlement T + 3	Trade appears as pending trade with value date 19/12/02
8/5/02	18/12/02 (2)	No action	N/A
13/5/02	19/12/02 (3)	Check failed trade reports	Trade does not appear on failed trade report
16/5/02	20/12/02 (4)	Check failed trade reports	Trade is reported on failed trade report

'Actual day' refers to the date the test business day is to be run and will often span more than one elapsed day as in this example. Notice that the one test script involves three actions on different test business days and that in this particular case, there are no actions required on the second test business day – we move straight from the first to the third test business day. Notice also that the results of each action are verified to make sure no errors creep in before we reach our main test objective on day 4.

It is possible to combine several tests in a single script and we can see in the above example that we could have used this same scenario to check the pending trade report on the third logical business day. There are no hard and fast rules on this except to say that the more conditions you combine into one script, the more complex it becomes, the more difficult it is to control and the more likely you are to incur mistakes. At the end of the day it is a balance between being swamped by too many simple discrete scripts versus losing control over fewer but more complex integrated scripts.

UAT execution

In a large system, the number of test scripts can run to thousands so it is easy to see that the control and management of the test process presents quite a management challenge. Whether it is achieved through a specialist software package or a simple spreadsheet, the recording and scheduling of test scripts must be coordinated from a central point. There is likely to be a significant number of users running and checking various test scripts so it is imperative that things like change of business day, report running, system close, etc. are carefully communicated and synchronized with peoples' individual progress within their own testing schedule. For example, you don't want to close the system and move the test day on only to find that several transactions have not been completed. This may result in a lost day for those particular tests and necessitate complex reworking of test data to try to accommodate the test script in a subsequent run.

UAT is a high-pressure exercise with tight deadlines and inexperience in the systems use conspiring to make things go wrong before reaching the test objective itself. Many problems in UAT are caused by operator error as people struggle not only with the new applications but also with business functions they wouldn't necessarily carry out in their day-to-day jobs. This is why you need to do as much preparation and planning as possible so that when UAT commences, everyone can focus exclusively on operating and understanding the system rather than having to worry about creating complex test conditions.

Space does not permit us to go into the execution of UAT in too much detail but we have set out below some points to bear in mind when conducting UAT:

- All test parameters and scripts should be completed and logged before testing commences.
- Transaction scripts should be clearly assigned to their requisite business day.
- The action and result of each transaction script execution should be logged centrally so that progress can be monitored and test results evaluated.
- Screen prints should be taken of all input/enquiry activity to aid debugging.
- Error messages should be carefully noted and supporting data values obtained for investigation purposes.
- Users should not try to debug errors but ensure they have sufficient evidence to hand over to IT – they should, however, check for possible operator error.
- Statistics should be kept on test script success rates to give a quantitative measure of system quality.

Users can be tempted to start investigating the internals of the system to try to resolve problems themselves. Although they find it very interesting, it only serves to slow down overall progress that eventually leads to scripts being missed from test runs and consequently prevents other errors being detected. Debugging errors is best left to the IT experts who have an intimate knowledge of the inner workings of the system and who can track down the problem much more efficiently. The primary responsibility of the users is to detect errors, not to fix them.

Performance testing

In addition to the testing stages already mentioned, you will sometimes encounter a further test stage known as performance testing which is about making sure the system can handle the workload of the business. It is generally carried out around the same time as user acceptance testing when the functionality is bedded down and it can be tested on its ability to handle average and peak workloads. The performance testing stage is not designed to test functionality but is concerned only with making sure that the functions can cope with the volume and time constraints of the business operating environment. To that end, performance testing will need to be carried out on a representative cross-section of system functionality with particular emphasis placed on those functions where throughput is critical. Performance testing will need to cover the following aspects of a system's operation:

- Number of static and transaction records that can be held without degrading performance
- Average and peak number of transactions that can be processed in a given period of time
- Response times for transaction input/amendment/enquiry based on a full-sized database
- Response times for *ad hoc* queries and enquiry lists, based on a full-size database
- Number of concurrent users that can be supported with acceptable response times

The actual testing will normally be performed by IT as they will need to write software to simulate high transaction volumes and user workloads. However, Operations need to set the performance acceptance criteria against which the performance is to be measured. For example:

- New trade input response time never greater than 5 seconds and, on average, not greater than 3
- System must be able to accept up to 1000 new trades in any 15-minute period without backlogging
- System must be able to support 100 users updating the system concurrently
- Historic enquiries on full-size database of 1 million transactions must start to return results set in no more than 15 seconds

Avoid quoting transaction throughput criteria on a per-day basis as you will find transactions come through from the front office in concentrated batches. While your system may support 40 000 transactions **per day**, spread evenly over 8 hours, in reality, 30 000 of these trades will come through in the last 3 hours requiring an hourly throughput of 10 000 trades whereas the system supports only 5000. While the daily volume is the same, the system with an hourly throughput of 5000 trades will end up creating backlogs during the last few hours of trading leading to late reporting, confirmations, etc.

Lastly, it is essential that performance testing is carried out on as close to the final version of the system as possible. Small functional amendments can have an enormous impact on performance which, if not tested at the time, may not come to light until several months later when the system starts to fill up.

Regression testing

When bugs are found, you need to have a strategy for getting them fixed and retested while still continuing with the rest of the UAT programme. In an ideal world all tests would be rerun following any software changes as this is the only way you can be sure that the change has had no adverse effect on any other part of the system. The process of reperforming tests that have already been executed successfully is known in the trade as regression testing. The trouble is that UAT is not performed in an ideal world and we have things like deadlines and cost overruns to consider which preclude us from performing an indefinite number of regression tests. Again it is a question of priorities – is the risk of software failure more significant than missed deadlines and additional cost? Certainly in the case of, for example, air traffic control systems one would assume bug-free software has to be proved even at the expense of missed deadlines and extra cost. In financial operations we can afford a balance between a survivable level of bugs at an acceptable overrun of time and cost and so judgements have to be made based on relative risks.

We said that there are no absolute rules for when and when not to regression test but the following notes may help you come to the optimum decision:

- Set a threshold for the percentage of failed tests under which a full regression test is automatic – anything under at least 70%.
- If a failed test is isolated to one test business day then the test can be reperformed on the next test business day.
- If a failure has following dependencies on subsequent test business days then you really need to regression test that day.
- If a failure is on the periphery of the system such as a confirmation, settlement instruction, report, etc. then it can safely be retested on the next test business day.
- If a failure occurs at the start of the transaction life cycle, then that transaction is automatically rendered invalid for further tests and so needs to be rerun.
- Consider the criticality of the function failing – if it would cause only an inconvenience and providing there aren't too many of them, again you can afford to be more lenient.
- If a failure is going to create a non-integral state in the database then it should be fixed there and then.

There are no rules on when to regression test and if you get to your last business day and find an isolated error in the confirmation, you are not going to regression test the whole system. On the other hand, if you are near to the end of UAT and find major design changes are necessary to get the performance up to standard, then you may seriously consider a full regression test as the impact is likely to be significant. At the end of the day, Operations, in conjunction with IT, will need to assess the level of risk being run by not carrying out a full regression test and decide accordingly.

Conversion

Whether you are replacing an existing system or automating a manual process for the first time, you will need to carry out some form of conversion to get from the current to the replacement system and processes. We have included conversion after UAT because that is the sequence in which it is carried out but, as for UAT, you need to be planning it from the outset. As an extreme, but feasible, illustration consider the replacement of an old high-volume transaction-processing system which has accumulated millions of transactions over its lifetime. Apart from any other considerations, the physical time taken to convert that volume of transactions could run into days even before taking account of any problems along the way. Although the potential problem is very apparent, such issues can be put to one side in the excitement of developing the upgraded replacement system and come back to bite you when it is too late to do anything about it! Remember also that in the world of global markets, with the possible exception of Christmas and Easter, the maximum time you can afford to have the system down is over the weekend and even then there are many markets which open on Saturdays. By the time you allow for closing down the current system, taking backups, installing the new system and all the other preparatory work, you are probably looking at a maximum of 12 hours in which to complete the actual conversion.

One of the key responsibilities of Operations in any conversion is cleaning up the current environment. Unless the system is very small or is entirely manual, you are undoubtedly going to employ conversion software to map the current data to the new database formats and for the purposes of this discussion, we will assume that we do need to employ conversion software. It is an unfortunate fact that ageing systems that have been bent and twisted to accommodate new requirements over their lifetime start to lose their integrity as additional data items and coding values are introduced to support specific needs. Although not very desirable, it is manageable in the old system because the system itself has been moulded around these *ad hoc* data values. In addition to these software nuances, users are often guilty of entering data incorrectly and not maintaining it properly due to lack of procedures and system validation. Often old systems may contain data for information only, which has no impact on its processing logic but may be used by the new systems processing logic. Before conversion can take place, the old data must have its integrity restored to a uniform state from which it can be mapped to the new database structures. Depending on the current state of the data, this exercise can range in size from large to enormous and needs to be carried out in parallel with the system development so that, ideally, it is ready before UAT commences. This then allows you to run your conversion as part of the UAT process to make the live simulation even more realistic. The conversion process itself will invariably create some inconsistencies which will need to be cleaned up in the new system after implementation.

The only difference between the conversion software and the system itself is that the conversion software will be used only once. Its quality and accuracy, if anything, is more important than the system it is converting to because if your starting point is corrupted, your new system doesn't stand a chance. It is essential that the same rigour be applied to the UAT of conversion software as it is to the system itself.

While rigorous testing of the conversion process is essential, it is not enough on its own. Considering the enormity of what is happening, you are taking the books and records of the organization and converting them into a completely new format – you need to be 100% certain that the new records retain their same values and status. The whole process needs to be backed up with a control framework that will at least confirm that the overall value and meaning is maintained. Where possible it is better to use existing controls as these benefit from a proven track record and similar controls will have had to be incorporated into the new system as discussed earlier. Without creating additional software which itself may be flawed, you should be able to carry out some basic integrity checks. For example, you can compare your total pending trade number and values before and after conversion to ensure that none have been lost or their financial values corrupted. So although there may be other corruptions in the data, at least you can be sure that your financial position is consistent.

Depending on how you do the conversion, the financial accounts can be another good comparison point to verify financial integrity and you may even consider using new nominal accounts to facilitate such a check. Verification based on existing controls is very reassuring as they cannot have been influenced by the new software you are implementing whereas purpose-built control checks could be flawed themselves, thus clouding the underlying situation.

Implementation

This is the point when the new system is installed in the live systems environment and is used and relied upon for the day-to-day running of the business. There are several approaches to implementation which we will look at later but first, irrespective of how we implement, there is a lot of preparatory work that needs to be carried out in advance and we have summarized this below:

- You may need to notify your clients if they are going to be affected by the change – e.g. a new confirmation format.
- You may want to notify your clearing relationships even if they shouldn't see any change just in case things go wrong.
- If it is a large change, the regulators will want to be given advanced notice as will your external auditors who will need to sign it off.
- If you are introducing new computer-to-computer links with external parties, then you will want to involve them in some form of testing.
- Chose your implementation date to give yourself as much time as possible but avoiding external events that may disrupt staffing levels.
- Plan the implementation down to the last minute and fix a point of no return allowing plenty of time for back-out.
- Ask the business if they can reduce trading volumes in the lead-up to implementation to reduce conversion volumes.
- Make sure the old system is up to date and properly closed down before starting implementation.

- Install as much software as possible in advance and leave it dormant, particularly any desktop applications which can be time consuming to deploy.

- Make sure that you have plenty of infrastructure and desktop support on hand throughout implementation.

- Run a central control function to coordinate the myriad tasks that will need to be completed in the correct sequence, at the correct time, by a specific person.

- Conduct regular briefings to bring everyone up to date with progress.

Detailed planning down to a minute-by-minute level is absolutely key to a successful conversion. On the day, conversion will need to be centrally controlled and the schedule updated meticulously to reflect progress so that any deviation from plan is immediately apparent. For large conversions it is prudent to have 'dress rehearsals' to ensure that everybody knows what to do and to confirm timings.

Parallel running

This is a very risk-averse approach which involves running the current and new systems concurrently but with the firm's official books and records still on the current system. Live transactions are entered into both systems concurrently and the outputs compared for accuracy. It allows people to gain experience of the system in a much less pressured environment as it is the current system which is still running the firm. While it is a very low-risk approach to implementation, it comes at a cost:

- Because you are having to do virtually everything twice, you may need up to twice the number of staff.

- The additional work can overstretch staff leading to failures in the day-to-day operation.

- Previously unknown errors in the current system can confuse comparison of results – automatically assume that the new system is wrong.

- Additional cost of supporting an additional, near-production status system.
- If the new system contains significant additional functionality, then a direct comparison of the output will not be possible.

One of the pitfalls of the parallel-run approach is to implement systems which have not been thoroughly user acceptance tested which results in onerous and extended parallel running. Parallel running is not an alternative to comprehensive system and user testing but an additional measure to reduce the risk of system failure still further.

Phased implementation

A phased approach to implementing systems makes a lot of sense as it allows you to confine your exposure to a particular function or product. You can then concentrate your resources across a much smaller area providing significant extra support if things start to go wrong. It also gives you the opportunity to learn from any mistakes and incorporate corrective measures into subsequent phases. As you would expect, there are some negative aspects to consider:

- Operations staff may have their production work split across two systems.
- You may not be able to define a workable phasing due to consolidated reporting requirements.
- It is necessary to carry out multiple conversions, potentially increasing risk.
- Extra cost of running and supporting two production systems – unlike parallel running, both systems have production status.
- Management overhead of controlling two production environments.

As for the parallel run approach you must not view the phased approach to implementation as an alternative to thorough testing.

Big bang

The big bang approach is the simplest but at the same time the most risky approach to implementing systems. It is simple because it entails the switching on of the new and the switching off of the old systems simultaneously without the added complexity of maintaining two systems in parallel. If it goes well, it will require much less effort post-implementation as there will be no need for dual keying of data as in the case of parallel running nor will it be necessary to consolidate results from two separate system as in the case of the phased approach. These are certainly attractions and for relatively small implementations, where the consequences of failure are manageable, this is the *de facto* method. However, in a major system upgrade, not only is the risk of something going wrong that much greater to start with but the consequences of a failure may be unsustainable. If you are implementing a system for one particular product line then if there is a major failure, at least the damage will be limited to that particular line of business which, although very damaging, should not jeopardize the organization overall. On the other hand, if you are replacing a system covering all product lines, a serious failure will put the very existence of the organization itself at risk.

On the face of it, you would never contemplate using the big bang approach on any sizeable implementation that involved mission-critical systems because even though the chance of failure may be low, the impact of failure would be unmanageable. But if you have tested your system thoroughly and trained all your staff why should anything go wrong? There are two fundamental reasons why things may still go wrong even after the most comprehensive testing programme. First, it is impossible to simulate the production environment 100% because:

- UAT is based on a pre-planned business scenario taking place in a controlled environment, whereas live running is unplanned in an unpredictable environment.

■ UAT is carried out by staff specifically selected for their systems acumen and in the live environment the system will be used by many people not so ably qualified.

Second, potentially thousands of pieces of software and configuration parameters have to be installed in the production environment and the chances of one or two being wrong are quite high. It is therefore essential that some basic end-to-end testing is carried out in the production environment before releasing the system for general use. The aim of these tests is not to test logic but to verify that the system has been installed correctly. By running a representative sample of product-line transactions you would hope to pick up any missing pieces of software or incorrectly set configuration parameters because the effect should be fairly fundamental. Although many IT departments employ sophisticated version control software for releasing new software components into production, you will still be well advised to carry out your own sample implementation tests. This applies to whichever method of implementation you are following although it is much more critical with big bang because you have no fallback option.

Software testing is a complex process not least because it is not always absolutely clear exactly how it should behave in the first place. Much of the development process requires diverse individuals to interpret what is required and consequently from time to time you will get differences in their interpretations. Good communication between Operations and IT throughout the development life cycle is the most important ingredient for success as the more fluent the flow of information, the more likely it is that such misinterpretations will be uncovered.

Chapter 6

Technology risk

It goes without saying that the reliance on technology in today's financial markets is so great that technology risk is a massive issue for organizations. The reader can discern from the preceding chapters that the benefits that technology has brought to the industry have been very significant, shaping today's globalized business of raising capital, trading and investment. Without doubt the capacity that technology has generated has led to the large growth in volumes and the introduction of new and sophisticated products. As we know, it has also transformed the way in which operations perform their tasks, giving a wide range of benefits from dematerialized settlement to added-value client services. However, this radical transformation of the industry has been accompanied by the introduction of technology risk. This risk is, perhaps not surprisingly, a significant element in operational risk but how and why does technology risk arise?

Technology risk can arise in many ways. Take, for instance, an organization that invests in new technology, either new to the business or new to the marketplace. The risk here is that the technology may be untried and subsequently proves difficult to work with, fails to meet requirements or is unreliable in operation. Alternatively, a firm may create technology risk by underinvesting in technology so that the operational processes become increasingly affected by the inadequate and failing systems.

There is also the risk of technology-based projects taking longer to complete or being over-budget and, in some cases, there may be inadequate training of the teams supporting and using the technology. Elsewhere in the book we have commented on the dangers of projects being mismanaged and over-running and, of course, in extreme cases the projects may be shelved because the funding and/or time runs out – costly mistakes in monetary as well as competitive and risk terms.

Implementation itself can, of course, be a risk with everything from inadequate training to underestimation of converting data from the old to the new system and adequate controls to reconcile this process.

A former colleague, Amanat Hussain in a book called *Managing Operational Risk in Financial Markets*, published by Butterworth-Heinemann, gave some additional technology and system risk issues and some of these have been incorporated into the following list of risk issues:

- Errors in the development of software. The complex nature of the investment banking industry means that any support system would require complex algorithms or business rules to be developed. Unless there is comprehensive testing, there is a risk that the algorithms may be incorrectly programmed.
- Errors in formulae or mathematical models. The nature of some products like derivatives requires development of complex models for revaluation or margin purposes. New products are constantly being introduced and new models need developing or existing ones updated.
- The quality and availability of systems support can be a major issue and cause severe problems in the operations environment.
- Problems with static data input and maintenance affecting key processes like revaluations, expiry of products, corporate actions, etc.
- Failure in network or communication channels.
- Inadequate security over the system and its output.

We can look at some of these in more detail.

System risk

A core technology risk is system risk. The failure of a system to perform or to be reliable can have far-reaching implications for an organization. Recommendation 2 of The International Securities Services Association Recommendations 2000 illustrates the importance of systems in allowing the efficient and risk-managed environment for securities clearing and settlement by considering technology risk from the point of view of core processing. In commenting on securities systems in the clearing house/custodian/Central Securities Depository fields it states:

> **ISSA 2000 Recommendation 2**
>
> Securities systems must allow the option of network access on an interactive basis. They should cope with peak capacity without any service degradation, and have sufficient standby capabilities to recover operations in a reasonably short period within each processing day.

The considerations in formulating this recommendation were the market infrastructure and the impact from the technology perspective. Their findings were that market infrastructure will need to accommodate:

- Increasing volumes of traffic and volatility in markets
- Globalization of investment
- Emergence of electronic communication networks (ECNs) as virtual exchanges
- Demand for real-time settlement of stock and cash with a move to real time or rapid multiple batch intra-day settlement
- Demand for flexible processes allowing delivery versus delivery of stock both internally and across depositiories
- Longer hours of operation for trading and need to support 24-hour, 7-day week operations.

This is a major issue for the industry as initiatives like STP rely on the ability of the key market organizations to put in place the above.

From a technology perspective, this gives rise to:

- Utilities that serve multiple trading markets or platforms
- Systems that can accommodate surges in activity (in transaction processing and information transmission) without any degradation of service and response time
- Real-time process enabling interactive communication to facilitate intra-day traffic
- Linkage to the appropriate real-time cash settlement processes
- Adequate contingency and back-up, minimizing the risk of outages that could prevent the timely completion of settlements on the contracted date

Each of the above issues is significant to both the suppliers of the systems and the users. The risk of defaults and financial losses increases when settlement is delayed and clearing houses, CSDs and custodians cannot afford to have or interact with unreliable core systems.

As ISSA points out, this implies that the technology infrastructure must have:

- Open access to on- and off-exchange markets
- Scaleable systems covering the maximum forecast daily volumes
- Resilient and fault-tolerant processes
- Continuous processing capability with interactive user communication links
- Adequate stand-by allowing for recovery of operations, without any loss of data in a reasonably short period within the working day

Operations managers will be familiar with the problems created by system downtime. It is a source of concern to risk managers as well, not least because the dealing activity cannot realistically be suspended every time the operations systems are down, even though it is not possible during this time to verify totally the exposure of the business. When we talk about system risk we need to differentiate between the internal system risk and the external risk as described in the ISSA Recommendations, and yet both are very significant issues in different ways.

Internal system risk

This is a risk that to some extent at least is under the control of the firm. The system is either in-house or supplied and may be supported internally or externally or both. It is chosen to meet the business requirement of the firm and developed accordingly. The risk associated with it would be:

- Capability to meet current and future levels of business
- Ability to handle products
- Age of system and reliability
- Poor maintenance capability
- Understanding of the scope of the system by operations managers and teams
- Comparison to other systems

When considering the degree of system risk it has, a firm must pay particular attention to these risk situations and be satisfied that the business is not being compromised as a result. If any are evident then the operational risk level is going to be increased, if the impact of any is compromising the clearing and settlement processes then the risk level is likely to be, or will become, critical. As a result, systems will need to be reviewed then redeveloped or replaced.

External system risk

The principal problem with external risk is that the firm is not very often in control, i.e. they have to utilize the system or services in any case. It is this impact of systems in the counterparty that worries ISSA and led to their recommendations.

The failure of systems within counterparties, whether they be prolonged failures or just inadequate functionality has a profound impact on the performance of the operations team within the user. For instance, the inability to provide timely and accurate data from a custodian has an impact on the client, likewise the inability of a CSD to receive and process correctly instructions. However, the problem is not just with the organizations within the clearing and settlement infrastructure, it also lies with the suppliers of systems to the banks, brokers and institutional clients.

Late delivery of system releases, errors in newly released functionality and failure to rectify errors with software in a timely fashion can all have a drastic affect on the operations team's ability to carry out the function efficiently. This in turn increases the risk. Monitoring of the system and support performance is therefore essential and while service level agreements may give some comfort they do not remove or negate all the risk.

System security

With systems and technology at the heart of the industry and the businesses it is not surprising that system security is considered a major operational risk. Fraud, money laundering, manipulation of data, technology criminals, terrorism and 'for fun' hackers all present a very real danger to businesses. In many cases the business is vulnerable because of poor security over access and/or availability of data output from the system.

Operations managers have a responsibility to ensure that the data input and output to and from the systems is in a controlled environment. This may seem very simple but in reality can actually be very difficult as the need to be able to carry out the processing functions can create areas where there is a conflict of interest with risk control. For example, it is late in the day and a new product has been traded that needs to be set up on the system. The natural control to prevent fraud would be to have an independent person from deal input/processing set up the product on the system. This would incorporate an independent check that the product was duly authorized etc. However, if this person (and any support) is not available or they are not competent to set up the product on the system there will be problems. As a result of not being set up or set up incorrectly the trade may not be processed, affecting records and reporting, and could affect clients and generate both operational and possibly regulatory risk.

However, if the processing team are permitted to set up products in the system there is a different, but just as dangerous, weakness. Organizations overcome this by sometimes having static data teams and manage the situation through ensuring availability of trained staff and setting deadlines for the time to set up a new product in the system. By instituting adequate procedures and controls the situation can be managed but incorporating this into headcount, operational hours and ensuring adequate competency is not easy, particularly in smaller firms.

On a more simplistic but nevertheless important note, password control into systems can be, and often is, woeful. Not only are passwords often freely shared, but they can take an age to be disabled after a person leaves the organization. Slack access rules open up an organization to all manner of dangers that, to be fair, the operations team member may not recognize. We have probably all used someone else's access code to expedite a quick solution to an inquiry, particularly when dealing with a client inquiry and they are waiting on the telephone for the reply. However, this cannot, in risk terms, be justified. The situation where the access code of a departed employee takes days, sometimes weeks, to be disabled is a totally unacceptable risk.

Problems also exist today with so many organizations offering and taking services via the Internet. Without question this is a quick and very attractive medium to communicate and get information, for instance from exchanges. However, unless there are adequate controls and protection to the systems a disaster is waiting to happen. It may be unsavoury that employees might access and download pornography, but the real danger is the vulnerability to viruses and hackers. Activists for various anti-capitalist groups, criminals and terrorists can bring a company quickly to its knees if they can access the core systems. With people often on the inside, i.e. employed in the firm, any weakness that can be discovered and then conveyed to compatriots on the outside presents a massive risk.

Business-continuation risk

With the exception of a regulatory suspension or ban, nowhere is there more risk to the continuation of the business than technology. If we look back at some of the risks we have already mentioned, most of them could manifest themselves into a very significant problem, some quite quickly. A virus, for instance, or a major problem with the implementation of a new system would be examples. Yet it is the loss or severe disruption of a system that perhaps creates the greatest concern in many people's minds. In London businesses have faced the threat of terrorism for many years and the Irish Republican Army (IRA) has, while never stopping the financial markets, or indeed firms operating in the markets, from continuing their business, given insight into the consequences of losing infrastructure like buildings. Although the threat from the IRA has to some extent been reduced by the Northern Ireland peace process, dissidents still harbour ideas about attacks on Britain and crave the publicity that a 'big one', i.e. bomb, brings. This was highlighted in the USA and indeed the world by the terror attacks of 11 September 2001. In both cases despite appalling destruction, deaths and damage, most businesses defiantly survived and continue in operation today. They did so because of disaster recovery and business-continuation policies that enabled them to re-establish the business, including systems, in an alternative location.

These types of massive disruption are a risk, there can be no question about that, and yet other potentially equally dangerous situations to the business exist.

As technology advances so the industry moves forward. Many key players in the infrastructure of the capital markets are coming together in mergers and alliances, changing the whole way in which business, including clearing and settlement, is carried out. As the systems move forward in the drivers we talked about earlier in the book take effect, some firms are caught in a very difficult situation. Redeveloping or replacing systems is neither cheap nor particularly easy to implement and yet a failure to modernize the systems can have massive implications for the business. On the one hand, there is the possibility of being unable to meet exchange or clearing house interface capabilities and therefore being unable to continue as a member of that organization. On the other, operations teams faced with increasing demands from clients for ever more sophisticated technology-based services cannot compete with other firms because of outdated systems.

These both pose significant threats to the firm and need to be addressed by a long-term commitment simply because the pace of change is unlikely to slow and 'temporary patches' are no solution.

Operations managers must therefore be very aware of their role in helping to plan and develop the system capabilities for the firm, as wrong decisions on the choice of system and the future requirements are not just simply an embarrassment and a financial loss, they may be terminal and prompt the firm to consider outsourcing the operations function. Given the threat to the business of the failure of systems to be adequate from a business and regulatory aspect, one can see why the directors may decide that the risk to the continuation of the business is too great, not to mention the investment, to maintain an Operations function.

There are, of course, many sound arguments for investing in systems and utilizing the Operations function as a revenue generator and support service to the business and its clients. So providing the Operations managers can show their ability to manage systems, both in usage and development capacity, there is no reason to believe that business-continuation risk cannot be adequately managed.

Summary

Technology risk is a significant part of operational risk and Operations managers must be aware of this and be professional in their management of it. It is also important to make sure that employees in the Operations teams understand technology risk and its potential impact.

Systems and technology provide the foundations for the kind of globalized industry we see today and yet they do not do so without risk to the participants. Technology risk will not go away and must therefore be recognized and managed by both suppliers and users. Any organization that fails to do so will sooner or later suffer a catastrophic loss or have their business activities curtailed by regulators or competitors.

Technology is power. It is also a risk.

Chapter 7

Trends and developments

Introduction

Throughout this book we have looked at how technology has changed and as a result has re-engineered the way Operations work. Technology has advanced ever since the earliest computerized processes began to remove the manual and paper-intensive procedures that were found throughout the financial markets. As participation has broadened so volumes of transactions have grown and new products have been developed to meet the sophisticated requirements of the markets and their users. Technology has been both a driver and a constraint on the users of markets. On the one hand, it has allowed complex products and services to be offered by those firms with state-of-the-art systems. On the other, it has put some firms into a position of being marginalized as they have neither the technology nor resource to obtain the technology and associated skills. As a result there is more and more outsourcing of technology and of the products and services that rely on advanced technology capabilities. We have seen this, for example, in custody and in the development of prime broker services where firms faced with significant investment have taken the business decision to pull out of providing certain types of products.

Automation in clearing and settlement has changed the skills profile of Operations teams in much the same way as electronic markets have changed the skills profile of dealers. Today we have in many organizations exception management and client service products where before we had data input clerks and reconciliation teams. The impact of this automation has been to change the risk profiles of businesses so that operational risks are now technology based rather than manual error based. As STP projects reach completion the transfer of the manual to automation-based procedures becomes an implementation task for Operations teams that for a short period increases operational risk but thereafter creates more capacity.

Trends and developments

The process of markets that are currently open-outcry moving towards becoming electronic markets continues and is accompanied by mergers, take-overs and alliances that will have far-reaching consequences for how Operations teams are working and using technology in the future.

Rationalization of markets to electronic markets is being supplemented or are being supported by rationalization in clearing and settlement. We have seen how Clearstream and Euroclear are now linked directly into exchange/clearing house groupings, Clearstream with Deutsche Borse and Euroclear with Euronext. As the number of counterparties that a firm has or needs for its international and domestic business reduces and becomes more automated so the 'real' STP goal can be achieved.

The move towards T + 1, netting through central counterparties and advanced risk management techniques being needed to meet regulatory and business requirements, are all providing challenges for the system suppliers and the Operations teams. Automation of processes covering securities lending and borrowing, corporate actions, foreign exchange settlement, etc. are all fundamental to the Operations teams of tomorrow. Quite simply, the technology capability of Operations functions and the IT skills of Operations staff will be vital for a business to be successful in the future.

The cost of developing and maintaining systems capable of moving forward with the developments in the industry is not just a challenge for Operations managers in the users but is also a key factor for the system suppliers. The pressure is to develop new products and services for a changing and, to some extent for the large systems, a shrinking market. The consequences of system suppliers failing to achieve success is likely to see some suppliers drop out of the market. For the clients of those companies the result could be just as severe. Old technology will neither handle the future requirements or be cheap to replace, for many the answer will be strategic withdrawal from running Operations functions and outsourcing them instead. As we have said, this is already happening and can only increase as technology and the markets advance.

Elsewhere there are changes to the technology issue that are not specifically process based. Data protection is a crucial subject as contravention of the rights of individuals and corporates to confidentiality is a massive legal and business issue.

The holding or storage of data and subsequent use is governed by law. Operations teams are in possession of data related to clients in terms of both their positions and information about the client, including personal details such as address as well as banking. It is clearly obvious that managers must be (a) aware of the issues surrounding client data and (b) have devised procedures and educated staff in the primary issues related to such data.

The security over client data is partially an issue of access to the relevant areas of the database and partially about the procedures of distribution of data related to clients. As such, managers must ensure that prudent controls exist that will give adequate security but do not impact adversely on the day-to-day processes of the Operations teams. Access risk is part of technology risk in terms of operational risk.

Technology is both power and danger. It gives advantages that can be exploited and problems that can be devastating. It drives operations but can equally be a constraint and it can be costly if not managed correctly.

Of all the things that affect Operations performance, technology is the biggest friend and at the same a nightmare. Only the managers that embrace technology and have the vision to develop it will be prepared for the changes and challenges that Operations face in the coming years.

Technology drives businesses, Operations managers drive technology. Making it happen is the challenge.

Glossary

30/360   Also 360/360 or 30(E)/360. A day/year count convention assuming 30 days in each calendar month and a 'year' of 360 days; adjusted in America for certain periods ending on 31st-day of the month (and then sometimes known as 30(A)/360).

AAA   The highest credit rating for a company or asset – the risk of default is negligible.

Accrued interest   Interest due on a bond or other fixed income security that must be paid by the buyer of a security to its seller. Usual compensation: coupon rate of interest times elapsed days from prior interest payment date (i.e. coupon date) up to but not including settlement date.

Actual settlement date   Date the transaction effectively settles in the clearing house (exchange of securities eventually against cash).

Add-on   In capital adequacy calculations, the extra capital required to allow for the possibility of a deal moving into profit before a mark-to-market calculation is next made.

Affirmation   Affirmation refers to the counterparty's agreement with the terms of the trade as communicated.

Agent   One who executes orders for or otherwise acts on behalf of another (the principal) and is subject to its control and authority. The agent takes no financial risk and may receive a fee or commission.

Agent bank   A commercial bank that provides services as per their instructions.

Allocation (give up)   The process of moving the trade from the executing broker to the clearing broker in exchange-traded derivatives.

Amortization Accounting procedure that gradually reduces the cost value of a limited life asset or intangible asset through periodic charges to income. The purpose of amortization is to reflect the resale or redemption value. Amortization also refers to the reduction of debt by regular payments of interest and principal to pay off a loan by maturity.

Annuity For the recipient, an arrangement whereby the individual receives a pre-specified payment annually for a pre-specified number of years.

Ask price Price at which a market-maker will sell stock. Also known as the offer price.

Assets Everything of value that is owned or is due: fixed assets (cash, buildings and machinery) and intangible assets (patents and goodwill).

Assignment The process by which the holder of a short option position is matched against a holder of a similar long option position who has exercised his right.

Authentication agent A bank putting a signature on each physical bond to certify its genuineness prior to the distribution of the definitive bonds on the market.

Bank of England The UK's central bank which undertakes policy decided by the Treasury and determines interest rates.

Bankers' acceptance Short-term negotiable discount note, drawn on and accepted by banks which are obliged to pay the face value amount at maturity.

Bargain Another word for a transaction or deal. It does not imply that a particularly favourable price was obtained.

Base currency Currency chosen for reporting purposes.

Basis (gross) The difference between the relevant cash instrument price and the futures price. Often used in the context of hedging the cash instrument.

Basis (value or net) The difference between the gross basis and the carry.

Basis point (BP) A change in the interest rate of one hundredth of one per cent (0.01%). One basis point is written as 0.01 when 1.0 represents 1%.

Basis risk   The risk that the price or rate of one instrument or position might not move exactly in line with the price or rate of another instrument or position which is being used to hedge it.

BBA   British Bankers' Association.

Bear   Investor who believes prices will fall.

Bearer document   Documents which state on them that the person in physical possession (the bearer) is the owner.

Benchmark bond   The most recently issued and most liquid government bond.

Beneficial owner   The underlying owner of a security who has paid for the stock and is entitled to the benefits of ownership.

Bid   (a) The price or yield at which a purchaser is willing to buy a given security. (b) To quote a price or yield at which a purchaser is able to buy a given security.

Bilateral netting   A netting system in which all trades executed on the same date in the same security between the same counter-parties are grouped and netted to one final delivery versus payment.

Bill of exchange   A money market instrument.

BIS   Bank for International Settlements.

Block trade   A purchase or sale of a large number of shares or dollar value of bonds normally much more than what constitutes a round lot in the market in question.

Bond   A certificate of debt, generally long-term, under the terms of which an issuer contracts, *inter alia*, to pay the holder a fixed principal amount on a stated future date and, usually, a series of interest payments during its life.

Bonus issue   A free issue of shares to a company's existing shareholders. No money changes hands and the share price falls pro rata. It is a cosmetic exercise to make the shares more marketable. Also known as a capitalization or scrip issue.

Book entry transfer   System of recording ownership of securities by computer where the owners do not receive a certificate. Records are kept (and altered) centrally in 'the book'.

Books closed day   Last date for the registration of shares or bonds for the payment of the next.

Break A term used for any out-of-balance condition. A money break means that debits and credits are not equal. A trade break means that some information such as that from a contra broker is missing to complete that trade.

Broker/dealer Any member firm of the Stock Exchange except the specialists which are GEMMs and IDBs.

Broken date A maturity date other than the standard ones normally quoted.

Broken period A period other than the standard ones normally quoted.

Broking The activity of representing a client as agent and charging commission for doing so.

Bull Investor who believes prices will rise.

Buying in The action taken by a broker failing to receive delivery of securities from a counterparty on settlement date to purchase these securities in the open market.

Call deposits Deposits which can be called (or withdrawn) at the option of the lender (and in some cases the borrower) after a specified period. The period is short, usually one or two days, and interest is paid at prevailing short-term rates (call account).

Call option An option that gives the seller the right, but not the obligation, to buy a specified quantity of the underlying asset at a fixed price, on or before a specified date. The buyer of a call option has the obligation (because they have bought the right) to make delivery of the underlying asset if the option is exercised by the seller.

Callable bond A bond that the issuer has the right to redeem prior to maturity by paying some specified call price.

Capital adequacy Requirement for firms conducting investment business to have sufficient funds.

Capital markets A term used to describe the means by which large amounts of money (capital) are raised by companies, governments and other organizations for long-term use and the subsequent trading of the instruments issued in recognition of such capital.

Capitalization issue *See* **Bonus issue**.

CASCADE   Name of the settlement system used by Clearstream for German equity settlement.

Cash market   A term used to describe the market where the cash asset trades, or the underlying market when talking about derivatives.

Cash sale   A transaction on the floor of the stock exchange which calls for delivery of the securities that same day. In 'regular way' trades, the seller delivers securities on the fifth business day.

Cash settlement   In the money market a transaction is said to be made for cash settlement if the securities purchased are delivered against payment on the same day the trade is made.

Central securities depository   An organization which holds securities in either immobilized or dematerialized form thereby enabling transactions to be processed by book entry transfer. Also provides securities administration services.

Certificate of deposit   A money market instrument.

CFTC   The Commodities and Futures Commission, (United States).

Chaps   Clearing House Automated Payment System – clearing system for sterling and Euro payments between banks.

Cheapest to deliver   The cash security that provides the lowest cost (largest profit) to the arbitrage trader; the cheapest to deliver instrument is used to price the futures contract.

Clean price   The total price of a bond less accrued interest.

Clearance   The process of determining accountability for the exchange of money and securities between counterparties to a trade: clearance creates statements of obligation for securities and/or funds due.

Clearance broker   A broker who will handle the settlement of securities related transactions for himself or another broker. Sometimes small brokerage firms may not clear for themselves and therefore employ the services of an outside clearing broker.

Clearing   The centralized process whereby transacted business is recorded and positions are maintained.

Clearing house   Company that acts as central counterparty for the settlement of stock exchange transactions. For example, on TD,

Broker X sold 100, 300 and 500 securities ABC and purchased 50 and 200 units of the same issue. The clearing system will net the transactions and debit X with 650 units ($-900 + 250 = 650$) against the total cash amount. This enables reduction of the number of movements and thus the costs.

Clearing organization   The clearing organization acts as the guarantor of the performance and settlement of contracts that are traded on an exchange.

Clearing system   System established to clear transactions.

Clearstream   CSD and clearing house based in Luxembourg and Frankfurt.

Closing day   In a new bond issue, the day when securities are delivered against payment by syndicate members participating in the offering.

Closing trade   A bought or sold trade which is used to partly offset an open position, to reduce it or to fully offset it and close it.

CMO   Central Moneymarkets Office – clearing house and depository for UK money markets.

Collateral   An acceptable asset used to cover a margin requirement.

Commercial paper   A money market instrument.

Commission   Charge levied by a firm for agency broking.

Commodity futures   These comprise five main categories: agriculturals (e.g. wheat and potatoes); softs (e.g. coffee and cocoa); precious metals (e.g. gold and silver); non-ferrous metals (e.g. copper and lead); and energies (e.g. oil and gas).

Common stock   Securities which represent ownership in a corporation. The two most important common stockholder rights are the voting right and dividend right. Common stockholders' claims on corporate assets are subordinate to those of bondholders; preferred stockholders and general creditors.

Compliance officer   Person appointed within an authorized firm to be responsible for ensuring compliance with the rules.

Compound interest   Interest calculated on the assumption that interest amounts will be received periodically and can be reinvested (usually at the same rate).

Conduct of Business Rules Rules required by FSA 1986 to dictate how firms conduct their business. They deal mainly with the relationship between firm and client.

Conflicts of interest Circumstances that arise where a firm has an investment which could encourage it not to treat its clients favourably. The more areas in which a firm is involved, the greater the number of potential conflicts.

Confirm An agreement for each individual OTC transaction which has specific terms.

Continuous net settlement Extends multilateral netting to handle failed trades brought forward. *See* **Multilateral netting**.

Contract The standard unit of trading for futures and options. It is also commonly referred to as a 'lot'.

Contract for difference Contract designed to make a profit or avoid a loss by reference to movements in the price of an item. The underlying item cannot change hands.

Contract note Legal documentation sent by a securities house to clients providing details of a transaction completed on their behalf.

Conversion premium The effective extra cost of buying shares through exercising a convertible bond compared with buying the shares directly in the market. Usually expressed as a percentage of the current market price of the shares.

Conversion price The normal value of a convertible which may be exchanged for one share.

Conversion ratio The number of shares into which a given amount (e.g. £100 or $1000) of the nominal value of a convertible can be converted.

Convertible bond Security (usually a bond or preferred stock) that can be exchanged for other securities, usually common stock of the same issuer, at the option of the holder and under certain conditions.

Convertible currency A currency that is freely convertible into another currency. Currencies for which domestic exchange control legislation specifically allows conversion into other currencies.

Corporate action One of many possible capital restructuring changes or similar actions taken by the company, which may have an impact on the market price of its securities, and which may require the shareholders to make certain decisions.

Corporate debt securities   Bonds or commercial papers issued by private corporations.

Correlation   Refers to the degree to which fluctuations of one variable are similar to those of another.

Cost of carry   The net running cost of holding a position (which may be negative), e.g. the cost of borrowing cash to buy a bond, less the coupon earned on the bond while holding it.

Counterparty   A trade can take place between two or more counterparties. Usually one party to a trade refers to its trading partners as counterparties.

Coupon   Generally, the nominal annual rate of interest expressed as a percentage of the principal value. The interest is paid to the holder of a fixed income security by the borrower. The coupon is generally paid annually, semi-annually or, in some cases quarterly depending on the type of security.

Credit risk   The risk that a borrower, or a counterparty to a deal, or the issuer of a security, will default on repayment or not deliver its side of the deal.

CREST   The organization in the UK that holds UK and Irish company shares in dematerialized form and clears and settles trades in UK and Irish company shares.

CRESTCo   Organization which owns CREST.

CREST member   A participant within CREST who holds stock in stock accounts in CREST and whose name appears on the share register. A member is their own user.

CREST sponsored member   A participant within CREST who holds stock in stock accounts in CREST and whose name appears on the share register. Unlike a member, a sponsored member is not their own user. The link to CREST is provided by another user who sponsors the sponsored member.

CREST user   A participant within CREST who has an electronic link to CREST.

Cross-border trading   Trading which takes place between persons or entities from different countries.

Cum-dividend   With dividend.

Cumulative preference share   If the company fails to pay a preference dividend the entitlement to the dividend accumulates and the arrears of preference dividend must be paid before any ordinary dividend.

Currency exposure   Currency exposure exists if assets are held or income earned, in one currency while liabilities are denominated in another currency. The position is exposed to changes in the relative values of the two currencies such that the cost of the liabilities may be increased or the value of the assets or earning decreased.

CUSIP   The Committee on Uniform Securities Identification Procedures, the body which established a consistent securities numbering system in the United States.

Custodian   Institution holding securities in safekeeping for a client. A custodian also offers different services to its clients (settlement, portfolio services, etc.).

Customer-non-private   Customer who is assumed to understand the workings of the investment world and therefore receives little protection from the Conduct of Business Rules.

Customer-private   Customer who is assumed to be financially unsophisticated and therefore receives more protection from the Conduct of Business Rules.

Day count fraction   The proportion of a year by which an interest rate is multiplied in order to calculate the amount accrued or payable.

Dealer   Individual or firm that acts as principal in all transactions, buying for their own account.

Default   Failure to perform on a futures contract, either cash settlement or physical settlement.

Deliverable basket   The list of securities which meets the delivery standards of futures contracts.

Delivery   The physical movement of the underlying asset on which the derivative is based from seller to buyer.

Delivery versus payment   Settlement where transfer of the security and payment for that security occur simultaneously.

Dematerialized (form)   Circumstances where securities are held in a book entry transfer system with no certificates.

Depository receipts   Certificate issued by a bank in a country to represent shares of a foreign corporation issued in a foreign country. It entitles the holder to dividends and capital gains. They trade and pay dividend in the currency of the country of issuance of the certificate.

Depository Trust Company (DTC)   A US central securities depository through which members may arrange deliveries of securities between each other through electronic debit and credit entries without the physical delivery of the securities. DTC is industry-owned with the NYSE as the majority owner and is a member of the Federal Reserve System.

Derivative   A financial instrument whose value is dependent upon the value of an underlying asset.

Dirty price   The total price of a bond including accrued interest.

Disclaimer   A notice or statement intending to limit or avoid potential legal liability.

Deutsche Börse   The German Stock Exchange.

Dividend   Distribution of profits made by a company if it chooses to do so.

Dividend per share   Indicated annual dividend based on the most recently announced quarterly dividend times four plus any additional dividends to be paid during the current fiscal year.

Dividend yield   The dividend expressed as a percentage of the share price.

DK   Don't Know. Applies to a securities transaction pending settlement where fundamental data are missing which prevents the receiving party from accepting delivery.

Domestic bond   Bond issued in the country of the issuer, in its country and according to the regulations of that country.

DTC   Depository Trust Company – CSD for shares in the USA.

ECB   European Central Bank.

ECSDA   European Central Securities Depository Association.

EFP   Exchange of futures for physical. Common in the energy markets. A physical deal priced on the futures markets.

EUCLID   Communications system operated by Euroclear.

EUREX German–Swiss derivatives exchange created by the merger of the German (DTB) and Swiss (SOFFEX) exchanges.

EURONEXT A Pan-European exchange incorporating the Dutch, French, Portuguese and Belgium Exchanges and LIFFE.

Earnings per share (EPS) The total profit of a company divided by the number of shares in issue.

Equity A common term to describe stocks or shares.

Equity/stock options Contracts based on individual equities or shares. On exercise of the option the specified amount of shares are exchanged between the buyer and the seller through the clearing organization.

E-T-D This is the common term which is used to describe exchange-traded derivatives which are the standardized products. It also differentiates products which are listed on an exchange as opposed to those offered Over-The-Counter.

EURIBOR A measure of the average cost of funds over the whole euro area based on a panel of 57 banks.

Eurobond An interest-bearing security issued across national borders, usually issued in a currency other than that of the issuer's home country.

Euroclear A book-entry clearing facility for most Eurocurrency and foreign securities. It is linked to EURONEXT.

European style option An option which can only be exercised on the expiry day.

Exception-based processing Transaction processing where straightforward items are processed automatically, allowing staff to concentrate on the items which are incorrect or not straight-forward.

Execution and clearing agreement An agreement signed between the client and the clearing broker. This agreement sets out the terms by which the clearing broker will conduct business with the client.

Exchange Marketplace for trading.

Exchange delivery settlement price (EDSP) The price deter-mined by the exchange for physical delivery of the underlying instrument or cash settlement.

Exchange-owned clearing organization   Exchange- or member-owned clearing organizations are structured so that the clearing members each guarantee each other with the use of a members' default fund and additional funding such as insurance, with no independent guarantee.

Exchange rate   The rate at which one currency can be exchanged for another.

Ex-date   Date on or after which a sale of securities is executed without the right to receive dividends or other entitlements.

Ex-dividend   Thirty-seven days before interest payment is due gilt-edged stocks are made 'ex-dividend'. After a stock has become 'ex-dividend', a buyer of stock purchases it without the right to receive the next (pending) interest payment.

Execution   The action of trading in the markets.

Execution and clearing agreement   An agreement signed between the client and the clearing broker. This sets out the terms by which the clearing broker will conduct business with the client.

Execution only or give-up agreement   Tripartite agreement which is signed by the executing broker, the clearing broker and the client. This sets out the terms by which the clearing broker will accept business on behalf of the client.

Exercise   The process by which the holder of an option may take up their right to buy or sell the underlying asset.

Exercise price (or strike price)   The fixed price, per share or unit, at which an option conveys the right to call (purchase) or put (sell) the underlying shares or units.

Expiry date   The last date on which an option holder can exercise their right. After this date an option is deemed to lapse or be abandoned.

Face value   The value of a bond, note, mortgage or other security that appears on the face of the issue, unless the value is otherwise specified by the issuing company. Face value is ordinarily the amount the issuing company promises to pay at maturity. It is also referred to as par or nominal value.

Failed transaction   A securities transaction that does not settle on time; i.e. the securities and/or cash are not exchanged as agreed on the settlement date.

Final settlement The completion of a transaction when the delivery of all components of a trade is performed.

Financial futures/options contracts Financial futures is a term used to describe futures contracts based on financial instruments such as currencies, debt instruments and financial indices.

Financial Services Authority (FSA) The agency designated by the Treasury to regulate investment business as required by FSA 1986 and then FSMA 2000. It is the main regulator of the financial sector and was formerly called the Securities and Investments Board (SIB). It assumed its full powers on 1 December 2001.

First notice day The first day that the holders of short positions can give notification to the exchange/clearing house that they wish to effect delivery.

Fiscal agent A commercial bank appointed by the borrower to undertake certain duties related to the new issue, such as assisting the payment of interest and principal, redeeming bonds or coupons, handling taxes, replacement of lost or damaged securities, destruction of coupons and bonds once payments have been made.

Fixed income Interest on a security which is calculated as a constant specified percentage of the principal amount and paid at the end of specified interest periods, usually annually or semi-annually, until maturity.

Fixed rate A borrowing or investment where the interest or coupon paid is fixed throughout the arrangement. In a FRA or coupon swap, the fixed rate is the fixed interest rate paid by one party to the other, in return for a floating-rate receipt (i.e. an interest rate that is to be refixed at some future time or times).

Fixed-rate borrowing This establishes the interest rate that will be paid throughout the life of the loan.

Flat position A position which has been fully closed out and no liability to make or take delivery exists.

Floating rate A borrowing or investment where the interest or coupon paid changes throughout the arrangement in line with some reference rate such as LIBOR. In a FRA or coupon swap, the floating rate is the floating interest rate (i.e. an interest rate that is to be refixed at some future time or times) paid by one party to the other, in return for a fixed-rate receipt.

Floating-rate note (FRN) Bond where each interest payment is made at the current or average market levels, often by reference to LIBOR.

Foreign bond Bond issued in a domestic market in the domestic currency and under the domestic rules of issuance by a foreign issuer (ex. Samurai bonds are bonds issued by issuers of other countries on the Japanese market).

Forex Abbreviation for foreign exchange (currency trading).

Forward delivery Transactions which involve a delivery date in the future.

Forward-rate agreements (FRAs) An agreement where the client can fix the rate of interest that will be applied to a notional loan or deposit, drawn or placed on an agreed date in the future, for a specified term.

Forwards These are very similar to futures contracts but they are not mainly traded on an exchange. They are not marked to market daily but settled only on the delivery date.

FSA Financial Services Authority.

FT-SE 100 index Main UK share index based on 100 leading shares.

Fund manager An organization that invests money on behalf of someone else.

Futures An agreement to buy or sell an asset at a certain time in the future for a certain price.

Gearing The characteristic of derivatives which enables a far greater reward for the same, or much smaller, initial outlay. It is the ratio of exposure to investment outlay, and is also known as leverage.

Gilt Domestic sterling-denominated long-term bond backed by the full faith and credit of the UK and issued by the Treasury.

Gilt-edged market-makers (GEMMs) A firm that is a market maker in gilts. Also known as a primary dealer.

Gilt-edged security UK government borrowing.

Give-up The process of giving a trade to a third party who will undertake the clearing and settlement of the trade.

Global clearing The channelling of the settlement of all futures and options trades through a single counterparty or through a number of counterparties geographically located.

Global custodian Institution that safekeeps, settles and performs processing of income collection, tax reclaim, multicurrency reporting, cash management, foreign exchange, corporate action and proxy monitoring etc. for clients' securities in all required marketplaces.

Global depository receipt (GDR) A security representing shares held in custody in the country of issue.

Good delivery Proper delivery of certificates that are negotiable and complete in terms of documentation or information.

Gross A position which is held with both the bought and sold trades kept open.

GSCC Government Securities Clearing Corporation – clearing organization for US Treasury securities.

Guaranteed bond Bonds on which the principal or income or both are guaranteed by another corporation or parent company in case of default by the issuing corporation.

Haircut The discount applied to the value of collateral used to cover margins.

Hedging A trading method which is designed to reduce or mitigate risk. Reducing the risk of a cash position in the futures instrument to offset the price movement of the cash asset. A broader definition of hedging includes using futures as a temporary substitute for the cash position.

Holder A person who has bought an open derivatives contract.

Immobilization The storage of securities certificates in a vault in order to eliminate physical movement of certificates/documents in transfer of ownership.

Independent clearing organization The independent organization is quite separate from the actual members of the exchange, and will guarantee to each member the performance of the contracts by having them registered in the organization's name.

Initial margin The deposit which the clearing house calls as protection against a default of a contract. It is returnable to the clearing member once the position is closed. The level is subject to changes in line with market conditions.

Institutional investor   An institution which is usually investing money on behalf of others. Examples are mutual funds and pension funds.

Interest rate futures   Based on a debt instrument such as a government bond or a Treasury bill as the underlying product and require the delivery of a bond or bill to fulfil the contract.

Interest rate swap   An agreement to exchange interest related payments in the same currency from fixed rate into floating rate (or vice versa) or from one type of floating rate to another.

Interim dividend   Dividend paid part-way through a year in advance of the final dividend.

International depository receipt (IDR)   Receipt of shares of a foreign corporation held in the vaults of a depository bank. The receipt entitles the holder to all dividends and capital gains. Dividends and capital gains are converted to local currency as part of the service. IDRs allow investors to purchase foreign shares without having to involve themselves in foreign settlements and currency conversion.

International equity   An equity of a company based outside the UK but traded internationally.

International petroleum exchange (IPE)   Market for derivatives of petrol and oil products.

International securities identification number (ISIN)   A coding system developed by the ISO for identifying securities. ISINs are designated to create one unique worldwide number for any security. It is a 12-digit alphanumeric code.

Interpolation   The estimation of a price or rate, usually for a broken date, from two other rates or prices, each of which is for a date either side of the required date.

Intra-day margin   An extra margin call which the clearing organization can call during the day when there is a very large movement up or down in the price of the contract.

Intrinsic value   The amount by which an option is in-the-money.

Investment services directive (ISD)   European Union Directive imposing common standards on investment business.

Investments   Items defined in the FSA 1986 to be regulated by it. Includes shares, bonds, options, futures, life assurance and pensions.

Invoice amount   The amount calculated under the formula specified by the futures exchange which will be paid in settlement of the delivery of the underlying asset.

IOSCO   International Organization of Securities Commissions.

IPMA   International Primary Markets Association.

Irredeemable gilt   A gilt with no fixed date for redemption. Investors receive interest indefinitely.

ISDA   International Swaps and Derivatives Association, previously known as the International Swap Dealers Association. Many market participants use ISDA documentation.

ISMA   International Securities Markets Association.

ISSA   The International Securities Services Association.

Issuer   Legal entity that issues and distributes securities.

Issuing agent   Agent (e.g. bank) who puts original issues out for sale.

JASDEC   Japan Securities Depository Centre – the CSD for Japan.

JSCC   Japan Securities Clearing Corporation – clearing organization in Japan.

Last notice day   The final day that notification of delivery of a futures contract will be possible. On most exchanges all outstanding short futures contracts will be automatically delivered to open long positions.

Last trading day   Often the day preceding last notice day which is the final opportunity for holders of long positions to trade out of their positions and avoid ultimate delivery.

LCH   London Clearing House.

Leverage   The magnification of gains and losses by only paying for part of the underlying value of the instrument or asset; the smaller the amount of funds invested, the greater the leverage. It is also known as gearing.

LIBID The London inter-bank bid rate. The rate at which one bank will lend to another.

LIBOR The London inter-bank offered rate. It is the rate used when one bank borrows from another bank. It is the benchmark used to price many capital market and derivative transactions.

LIFFE London International Financial Futures and Options Exchange.

Liquidity A liquid asset is one that can be converted easily and rapidly into cash without a substantial loss of value. In the money market, a security is said to be liquid if the spread between bid and asked price is narrow and reasonable size can be done at those quotes.

Liquidity risk The risk that a bank may not be able to close out a position because the market is illiquid.

Listed securities Securities listed on a stock exchange are tradeable on this exchange.

Loan stock *See* **Bond**.

London Inter-Bank Offered Rate (LIBOR) Rate at which banks lend to each other which is often used as the benchmark for floating rate notes (FRNs).

London International Financial Futures and Options Exchange (LIFFE) Market for trading in bond, interest rate, FT-SE 100 index and FTSE Mid 250 index, futures, plus equity options and soft commodity derivatives.

London Metal Exchange (LME) Market for trading in derivatives of metals such as copper, tin, zinc, etc.

London Stock Exchange (LSE) Market for trading in securities. Formerly known as the International Stock Exchange of the UK and Republic of Ireland or ISE.

Long A bought position in a derivative which is held open.

Long-dated Gilts with more than 15 years until redemption.

Long position Refers to an investor's account in which he has more shares of a specific security than he needs to meet his settlement obligations.

Lot The common term used to describe the standard unit of trading for futures and options. It is also referred to as a 'contract'.

Mandatory event   A corporate action which affects the securities without giving any choice to the security holder.

Margin   *Initial margin* is collateral placed by one party with a counterparty or clearing house at the time of a deal, against the possibility that the market price will move against the first party, thereby leaving the counterparty with a credit risk. *Variation margin* is a payment made, or collateral transferred, from one party to the other because the market price of the transaction or of collateral has changed. Variation margin payment is either in effect a settlement of profit/loss (for example, in the case of a futures contract) or the reduction of credit exposure. In a loan, margin is the extra interest above a benchmark such as LIBOR required by a lender to compensate for the credit risk of that particular borrower.

Mark-to-market   The process of revaluing an OTC or exchange-traded product each day. It is the difference between the closing price on the previous day against the current closing price. For exchange traded products this is referred to as variation margin.

Market   Description of any organization or facility through which items are traded. All exchanges are markets.

Market counterparty   A person dealing as agent or principal with the broker and involved in the same nature of investment business as the broker. This also includes fellow members of the FSA or trading members of an investment exchange for those products only where they are members.

Market-maker   A trader who works for an organization such as an investment bank. They quote bids and offers in the market and are normally under an obligation to make a price in a certain number of contracts. They create liquidity in the contract by offering to buy or sell.

Market price   In the case of a security, the market price is usually considered as the last reported price at which the stock or bond has been sold.

Market risk   Also position risk. The risk that the market value of a position falls.

Market value   The price at which a security is trading and could presumably be purchased or sold.

Master agreement   This agreement is for OTC transactions and is signed between the client and the broker. It covers the basic terms under which the client and broker wish to transact business. Each individual trade has a separate individual agreement with specific terms known as a confirm.

Matching (comparison)   Another term for comparison (or checking); a matching system to compare trades and ensure that both sides of trade correspond.

Maturity   The date on which the principal or nominal value of a bond becomes due and payable in full to the holder.

Medium dated   Gilts due to be redeemed within the next seven to fifteen years.

Model risk   The risk that the computer model used by a bank for valuation or risk assessment is incorrect or misinterpreted.

Modified following   The convention that if a settlement date in the future falls on a non-business day, the settlement date will be moved to the next following business day, unless this moves it to the next month, in which case the settlement date is moved back to the last previous business day.

Money market   The market for the purchase and sale of short-term financial instruments. Short term is usually defined as less than one year.

Money rate of return   Annual return as a percentage of asset value.

MOF   The Ministry of Finance (Japan).

Multilateral netting   Trade between several counterparties in the same security are netted such that each counterparty makes only one transfer of cash or securities to another party or to a central clearing system. Handles only transactions due for settlement on the same day.

Mutual collateralization   The deposit of collateral by both counterparties to a transaction.

NASDAQ   National Association of Securities Dealers Automated Quotation system.

Netting   Trading partners offset their positions thereby reducing the number of positions for settlement. Netting can be *bilateral, multilateral* or *continuous net settlement*.

Net asset value (NAV) In mutual funds, the market value of the fund share. It is common practice for an investment trust to compute its assets daily, or even twice a day, by totalling the closing market value of all securities and assets (i.e. cash) owned. All liabilities are deducted, and the balance is divided by the number of shares outstanding. The resulting figure is the net asset value per share.

Net present value (NPV) The net total of several present values (arising from cashflows at different future dates) added together, some of which may be positive and some negative.

Nil paid rights price Ex-rights price less the subscription price.

Nominal amount Value stated on the face of a security (principal value, par value). Securities processing: number of securities to deliver/receive.

Nominal value of a bond The value at which the capital, or principal, of a bond will be redeemed by the issuer. Also called par value.

Nominal value of a share The minimum price at which a share can be issued. Also called par value.

Nominee An organization that acts as the named owner of securities on behalf of a different beneficial owner who remains anonymous to the company.

Non-callable Cannot be redeemed by the issuer for a stated period of time from date of issue.

Non-clearing member A member of an exchange who does not undertake to settle their derivatives business. This type of member must appoint a clearing member to register all their trades at the clearing organization.

Non-cumulative preference share If the company fails to pay a preference dividend the entitlement to the dividend is simply lost. There is no accumulation.

Non-private customer A person who is not a private customer or who has requested to be treated as a non-private customer.

Nostro reconciliation Checking the entries shown on the bank's nostro account statement with the bank's internal records (the accounting ledgers) to ensure that they correspond exactly.

Note   Bonds issued with a relatively short maturity are often called notes.

Notional   Contracts for differences require a notional principal amount on which settlement can be calculated.

Novation   The process where registered trades are cancelled with the clearing members and substituted by two new ones – one between the clearing house and the clearing member seller, the other between the clearing house and the clearing member buyer.

NSCC   National Securities Clearing Corporation – clearing organization for US shares.

OASYS   Trade confirmation system for US brokers operated by Thomson Financial Services.

Obligation netting   An arrangement to transfer only the net amount (of cash or a security) due between two or more parties, rather than transfer all amounts between the parties on a gross basis.

Off-balance sheet   A transaction whose principal amount is not shown on the balance sheet because it is a contingent liability or settled as a contract for differences.

Offer price   The price at which a trader or market-maker is willing to sell a contract.

Offshore   Relates to locations outside the controls of domestic monetary, exchange and legislative authorities. Offshore may not necessarily be outside the national boundaries of a country. In some countries, certain banks or other institutions may be granted offshore status and thus be exempt from all or specific controls or legislation.

Omnibus account   Account containing the holdings of more than one client.

On-balance sheet   A transaction whose principal amount is shown on the balance sheet.

On-line   Processing which is executed via an interactive input onto a PC or stationary terminal connected to a processing centre.

Open outcry   The style of trading whereby traders face each other in a designated area such as a pit and shout or call their respective bids and offers. Hand signals are also used to communicate. It is governed by exchange rules.

Open interest   The number of contracts both bought and sold which remain open for delivery on an exchange. Important indicator for liquidity.

Open position   The number of contracts which have not been off-set at the clearing organization by the close of business.

Opening trade   A bought or sold trade which is held open to create a position.

Operational risk   The risk of losses resulting from inadequate systems and control, human errors or management failings.

Option   An option is in the case of the *buyer*; the right, but not the obligation, to take (call) or make (put) for delivery of the underlying product and in the case of the *seller*; the obligation to make or take delivery of the underlying product.

Option premium   The sum of money paid by the buyer for acquiring the right of the option. It is the sum of money received by the seller for incurring the obligation, having sold the rights, of the option. It is the sum of the intrinsic value and the time value.

Optional dividend   Dividend that can be paid either in cash or in stock. The shareholders entitled to the dividend make the choice.

Options on futures   These have the same characteristics as an option, the difference being that the underlying product is either a long or short futures contract. Premium is not exchanged, the contracts are marked to market each day.

Order-driven market   A stock market where brokers acting on behalf of clients match trades with each other either on the trading floor of the exchange or through a central computer system.

Out-of-pocket expenses   Market charges which are charged to the client without taking any profit.

Out-trade   A trade which has been incorrectly matched on the floor of an exchange.

Over-the-counter (OTC)   A one-to-one agreement between two counterparties where the specifications of the product are completely flexible and non-standardized.

Over-the-counter trading   Trading made outside a stock exchange.

Pair off   Back-to-back trade between two parties where settlement occurs only by exchanging the cash difference between the two parties.

Par value   *See* **Nominal value**.

Pari passu   Without partiality. Securities that rank *pari passu*, rank equally with each other.

Paying agent   A bank which handles payment of interest and dividends on behalf of the issuer of a security.

Payment date   Date on which a dividend or an interest payment is scheduled to be paid.

Perpetual bond   A bond which has no redemption date.

Portfolio   List of investments held by an individual or company, or list of loans made by a bank or financial institution.

Premium   An option premium is the amount paid upfront by the purchaser of the option to the writer.

Present value   The amount of money which needs to be invested (or borrowed) now at a given interest rate in order to achieve exactly a given cashflow in the future, assuming compound reinvestment (or refunding) of any interest payments received (or paid) before the end.

Pre-settlement   Checks and procedures undertaken immediately after execution of a trade prior to settlement.

Principal protected product   An investment whose maturity value is guaranteed to be at least the principal amount invested initially.

Principal-to-principal market   A market where the clearing house recognizes only the clearing member as one entity, and not the underlying clients of the clearing member.

Principal trading   When a member firm of the London Stock Exchange buys stock from or sells stock to a non-member.

Principal value   That amount inscribed on the face of a security and exclusive of interest or premium. It is the one used in the computation of interest due on such a security.

Private customer   An individual person who is not acting in the course of carrying on investment business.

Proprietary trader   A trader who deals for an organization such as an investment bank taking advantage of short-term price movements as well as taking long-term views on whether the market will move up or down.

Put option   An option that gives the buyer the right, but not the obligation, to sell a specified quantity of the underlying asset at a fixed price, on or before a specified date. The seller of a put option has the obligation (because they have sold the right) to take delivery of the underlying asset if the option is exercised by the buyer.

Quote driven   Dealing system where some firms accept the responsibility to quote buying and selling prices.

Range forward   A forward outright with two forward rates, where settlement takes place at the higher forward rate if the spot rate at maturity is higher than that, at the lower forward rate if the spot rate at maturity is lower than that, or at the spot rate at maturity otherwise.

RCH   Recognized clearing house under FSMA 2000.

Real-time gross settlement (RTGS)   Gross settlement system where trades are settled continuously through the processing day.

Realized profit   Profit which has arisen from a real sale.

Recognized investment exchange (RIE)   Status required by FSMA 2000 for exchanges in the UK.

Reconciliation   The comparison of a person's records of cash and securities position with records held by another party and the investigation and resolution of any discrepancies between the two sets of records.

Record date   The date on which a securities holder must hold the securities in order to receive an income or entitlement.

Redemption   The purchase and cancellation of outstanding securities through a cash payment to the holder.

Redemption price   A price at which bonds may be redeemed, or called, at the issuer's option, prior to maturity (often with a slight premium).

Registered bond   A bond whose owner is registered with the issuer or its registrar.

Registered title   Form of ownership of securities where the owner's name appears on a register maintained by the company.

Registrar   An official of a company who maintains its share register.

Registrar of companies Government department responsible for keeping records of all companies.

Replacement cost The mark-to-market loss which would be incurred if it were necessary to undertake a new transaction to replace an existing one, because the existing counterparty defaulted.

Repurchase agreement (repo) Borrowing funds by providing a government security for collateral and promising to 'repurchase' the security at the end of the agreed upon time period. The associated interest rate is the 'repo-rate'.

Reputational risk The risk that an organization's reputation will be damaged.

RIE Recognized investment exchange under FSA 1986.

Rights issue Offer of shares made to existing shareholders.

Right of offset Where positions and cash held by the clearing organization in different accounts for a member are allowed to be netted.

Risk warning Document that must be despatched and signed by private customers before they deal in traded options.

Roll-over A LIBOR fixing on a new tranche of loan, or transfer of a futures position to the next delivery month.

Rolling settlement System used in most countries including England. Bargains are settled a set number of days after being transacted.

Safekeeping Holding of securities on behalf of clients. They are free to sell at any time.

SCL Settlement organization and custodian of Spanish securities.

Scrip dividends Scrip dividends options provide shareholders with the choice of receiving dividend entitlements in the form of cash, shares or a combination of both. The amount of stocks to be distributed under a scrip option is calculated by dividing the cash dividend amount by the average market price over a recent period of time.

Scrip issue *See* **Bonus issue**.

SEATS Plus An order-driven system used on the London Stock Exchange for securities which do not attract at least two firms of market-makers and for all AIM securities.

Secondary market Marketplace for trading in existing securities. The price at which they are trading has no direct effect on the company's fortunes but is a reflection of investors' perceptions of the company.

Securities Bonds and equities.

Securities house General term covering any type of organization involved in securities although usually reserved for the larger firms.

Securities lending Loan of securities by an investor to another (usually a broker–dealer), usually to cover a short sale.

Securities and futures authority (SFA) Prior to the FSA assuming its full powers, it was the SRO responsible for regulating securities and futures firms.

Securities and investments board (SIB) Former name of the Financial Services Authority.

SEDOL Stock Exchange Daily Official List, a securities numbering system assigned by the International Stock Exchange in London.

Segregated account Account in which there is only the holdings of one client.

Segregation of funds Where the client's assets are held separately from those assets belonging to the member firm.

Self-regulating organizations (SROs) Bodies which receive their status from FSA and are able to regulate sectors of the financial services industry. Membership of an SRO provides authorization.

SEQUAL The checking system used for international equities.

SETS London Stock Exchange Trading System.

Settlement The fulfilment of the contractual commitments of transacted business.

Settlement date The date on which a trade is cleared by delivery of securities against funds (actual settlement date, contractual settlement date).

Share option A right sold to an investor conferring the option to buy or sell shares of a particular company at a predetermined price and within a specified time limit.

Short A sold position in a derivative which is held open.

Short coupons Bonds or notes with a short current maturity.

Short cover   The purchase of a security that has been previously sold short. The purpose is to return securities that were borrowed to make a delivery.

Short-dated gilt   Gilts due to be redeemed within the next seven years, according to the LSE (FT states up to 5 years).

Short sale   The sale of securities not owned by the seller in the expectation that the price of these securities will fall or as part of an arbitrage.

Short selling   Selling stock that you do not own.

Short-term security   Generally an obligation maturing in less than one year.

SICOVAM   CSD for French corporate securities and OATs (now merged with Euroclear).

Simple interest   Interest calculated on the assumption that there is no opportunity to reinvest the interest payments during the life of an investment and thereby earn extra income.

SIS   SEGA Inter Settle – CSD for Switzerland.

Soft commodities   Description given to commodities such as sugar, coffee and cocoa, traded through LIFFE since its incorporation of the former London Commodity Exchange (LCE).

Sovereign debt securities   Bonds issued by the government of a country.

SPAN   Standardized Portfolio Analysis of Risk. A form of margin calculation which is used by various clearing organizations.

Speculation   A deal undertaken because the dealer expects prices to move in his favour and thereby realize a profit.

Speculator   The speculator is a trader who wants to assume risk for potentially much higher rewards.

Sponsored member   Type of CREST member whose name appears on the register but has no computer link with CREST.

Spot delivery   A delivery or settlement of currencies on the value date, two business days later.

Spot market   Market for immediate as opposed to future delivery. In the spot market for foreign exchange, settlement is in two business days ahead.

Spot month   The first month for which futures contracts are available.

Spot rate   The price prevailing in the spot market.

Spread   (1) The difference between bid and asked price on a security. (2) Difference between yield on or prices of two securities of different types or maturities. (3) In underwriting, difference between price realized by an issuer and price paid by the investor. (4) Difference between two prices or two rates. What commodities traders would refer to as the basis.

Stamp duty   Tax on purchase of equities in the UK.

Stamp Duty Reserve Tax (SDRT) (UK)   Tax payable on the purchase of UK equities in uncertified form (i.e. those held within CREST).

Standard settlement instructions   Instructions for settlement with a particular counterparty which are always followed for a particular kind of deal and, once in place, are therefore not repeated at the time of each transaction.

Standing instruction   Default instruction, e.g. provided to an agent processing payments or clearing securities trades; provided by shareholder on how to vote shares (for example, vote for all management recommended candidates).

Stanza di compensazione   Italian clearing organization.

Stock   In some countries (e.g. the USA), the term applies to ordinary share capital of a company. In other countries (e.g. the UK), stock may mean share capital that is issued in variable amounts instead of in fixed specified amounts, or it can describe government loans.

Stock dividend   Dividends paid by a company in stock instead of cash.

Stock Exchange Automated Quotation System (SEAQ)   Electronic screen display system through which market-makers in equities display prices at which they are willing to deal.

Stock Index Futures/Options   Based on the value of an underlying stock index such as the FTSE 100 in the UK, the S&P 500 index in the USA and the Nikkei 225 and 300 in Japan. Delivery is fulfilled by the payment or receipt of cash against the exchange calculated delivery settlement price. These are referred to as both indices or indexes.

Stock (order) An owner of a physical security that has been mutilated, lost or stolen will request the issuer to place a stop (transfer) on the security and to cancel and replace the security.

Stock (or bond) power A legal document, either on the back of registered stocks and bonds or attached to them, by which the owner assigns his interest in the corporation to a third party, allowing that party the right to substitute another name on the company records instead of the original owner's.

Stock split When a corporation splits its stock, it divides.

Straight debt A standard bond issue, without right to convert into the common shares of the issuer.

Straightthrough processing Computer transmission of the details of a trade, without manual intervention, from their original input by the trader to all other relevant areas – position keeping, risk control, accounts, settlement, reconciliation.

Street name Securities held in street name are held in the name of a broker or another nominee, i.e. a customer.

Strike price The fixed price, per share or unit, at which an option conveys the right to call (purchase) or put (sell) the underlying shares or units.

Strike price/rate Also exercise price. The price or rate at which the holder of an option can insist on the underlying transaction being fulfilled.

Stripped bonds (strips) Bonds where the rights to the interest payments and eventual repayment of the nominal value have been separated from each other and trade independently. Facility introduced for gilts in December 1997.

Sub-custodian A bank in a foreign country that acts on behalf of the custodian as its custody agent.

Subscription price Price at which shareholders of a corporation are entitled to purchase common shares in a rights offering or at which subscription warrants are exercisable.

Subscriptions In a bond issue, the buying orders from the lead manager, co-managers, underwriters and selling group members for the securities being offered.

Stump period   A calculation period, usually at the beginning or end of a swap, other than the standard ones normally quoted.

Swap   Arrangement where two borrowers, one of whom has fixed interest and one of whom has floating rate borrowings, swap their commitments with each other. A bank would arrange the swap and charge a fee.

SwapClear   A clearing house and central counterparty for swaps.

SwapsWire   An electronic dealing system for swaps.

SWIFT   Society for Worldwide Interbank Financial Telecommunications – secure electronic communications network between banks.

TARGET   Trans European Automated Real time Gross settlement Express Transfer – system linking the real-time gross settlements for euros in the 15 European Union countries.

Tax reclaim   The process that a global custodian and/or a holder of securities performs, in accordance with local government filing requirements, in order to recapture an allowable percentage of tax withheld.

Termination date   The end date of a swap.

Thomson Report   An electronic transaction reporting system for international equities on the London Stock Exchange operated by Thomson.

Tick size   The value of a one-point movement in the contract price.

Time value   The amount by which an option's premium exceeds its intrinsic value. Where an option has no intrinsic value the premium consists entirely of time value.

Trade date   The date on which a trade is made.

Trade guarantees   Guarantees in place in a market which ensure that all compared or netted trades will be settled as compared regardless of a counterparty default.

Traded option   An option which is traded on an exchange.

Trader   An individual who buys and sells securities with the objective of making short-term gains.

Transfer agent   Agent appointed by a corporation to maintain records of stock and bond owners, to cancel and issue certificates and to resolve problems arising from lost, destroyed or stolen certificates.

Transfer form   Document which owners of registered documents must sign when they sell the security. Not required where a book entry transfer system is in use.

Transparency   The degree to which a market is characterized by prompt availability of accurate price and volume information which gives participants comfort that the market is fair.

TRAX   Trade confirmation system for the Euromarkets operated by ISMA.

Treasury bill   Money market instrument issued with a life of less than one year issued by the US and UK governments.

Treasury bonds (USA)   US government bond issued with a 30-year maturity.

Treasury notes (USA)   US government bond issued with 2-, 3-, 5- and 7-year maturity.

Triple A rating   The highest credit rating for a bond or company – the risk of default (or non-payment) is negligible.

Trustee   A person appointed to oversee the management of certain funds. They are responsible for ensuring that the fund is managed correctly and that the interests of the investor are protected and that all relevant regulations and legislation are complied with.

Turnaround   Securities bought and sold for settlement on the same day.

Turnaround time   The time available or needed to settle a turnaround trade.

Underlying asset   The asset from which the future or option's price is derived.

Undersubscribed   Circumstance when people have applied for fewer shares than are available in a new issue.

Unrealized profit   Profit which has not arisen from a sale – an increase in value of an asset.

Value at Risk (VaR)   The maximum amount which a bank expects to lose, with a given confidence level, over a given time period.

Variation margin   The process of revaluing an exchange-traded product each day. It is the difference between the closing price on the previous day against the current closing price. It is physically paid or received each day by the clearing organization. It is often referred to as the mark-to-market.

Volatility   The degree of scatter of the underlying price when compared to the mean average rate.

Warrant   An option which can be listed on an exchange, with a lifetime of generally more than one year.

Warrant agent   A bank appointed by the issuer as an intermediary between the issuing company and the (physical) warrant holders, interacting when the latter want to exercise the warrants.

Withholding tax   In the securities industry, a tax imposed by a government's tax authorities on dividends and interest paid.

Writer   A person who has sold an open derivatives contract and is obliged to deliver or take delivery upon notification of exercise from the buyer.

XETRA   Dealing system of the Deutsche Börse.

Yield   Internal rate of return expressed as a percentage.

Yield curve   For securities that expose the investor to the same credit risk, a graph showing the relationship at a given point in the time between yield and current maturity. Yield curves are typically drawn using yields on governments of various maturities.

Yield to maturity   The rate of return yielded by a debt security held to maturity when both interest payments and the investor's capital gain or loss on the security are taken into account.

Zero coupon bond   A bond issued with no coupon but a price substantially below par so that only capital is accrued over the life of the loan, and yield is comparable to coupon-bearing instruments.

Index

SECURITIES INSTITUTE

Qualifications

Securities Institute Diploma –
the professional qualification for
practitioners leading to Fellowship
of the Institute

Investment Advice Certificate –
the benchmark examination for
financial advisors

**SFA Registered Persons
Examination** – the benchmark
examinations for employees of SFA
regulated firms

**Investment Administration
Qualification** – the benchmark
examination for administration,
operations and IT staff

**International Capital Markets
Qualification** – the introductory
qualification for overseas and
emerging markets

Membership

Professionalism through a
progressive structure of recognised
designations: SIAff, MSI, FSI

Over 17,000 students, affiliates,
members and fellows

**Free membership events,
providing education and
networking opportunities**

Examination qualification
programmes

**Continuing Learning
opportunities** through a wide
range of courses and conferences
with discounts available for
members

Training, Continuing Learning & Publications for the financial services industry

The courses, seminars and publications we produce are researched and
developed by working closely with market practitioners and employers
to produce focussed, high quality and value-for-money training
solutions that meet the needs of busy professionals.

To find out more about all our products and services, please call the
Marketing Department on *020 7645 0670,*
email us on *marketing@securities-institute.org.uk,*
or visit our web site:

www.securities–institute.org.uk

Centurion House, 24 Monument Street, London, EC3R 8AQ

PROFESSIONALISM | INTEGRITY | EXCELLENCE